$2.50

Selected Sermon Outlines

SELECTED
SERMON OUTLINES

Compiled by
CHARLES O. STRONG
Professor of Homiletics,
Central Baptist College, Conway, Arkansas

ZONDERVAN PUBLISHING HOUSE
GRAND RAPIDS, MICHIGAN

DEDICATION

To

those gracious people who have tolerated my preaching since 1941

AND TO

those preachers who have sat in my speech classes since 1954.

PREFACE

Originality is not claimed for these contents. These outlines were gleaned from classes at Columbia Baptist Bible School, Magnolia, Arkansas; Jacksonville College, Jacksonville, Texas; East Texas Baptist College, Marshall, Texas; from many of my preacher brethren; and from private study.

If I remembered where I got the outline, the appropriate initials have been affixed. I cannot vouch for its original source; you may find one of yours here with the initials of another on it.

These are outlines that the editor has used in several pastorates and revival efforts. No effort has been made to make the outlines expansive or explanatory. Study will be required to make them meaningful and useful. No preacher can afford to attempt to preach without personal preparation.

This first effort is sent forth with the sincerest prayer that it shall prove of some blessing to those who use it and to those who have to listen to it.

CHARLES O. STRONG

INTRODUCTION

It is with the greatest of pleasure that I write a brief introduction to *Selected Sermon Outlines* by my good friend and fellow instructor and minister of the Gospel. I consider him well qualified for the task he assumed in getting together this book of sermon outlines. He does not claim originality for all of them, though he is, in my estimation, qualified to prepare a book of original outlines.

I have read most of the outlines in this book, and I consider them sound, sensible, and safe. They should be a great help, especially to preachers just beginning the work of the ministry of the Gospel of our Lord Jesus Christ. The outlines, however, will require study on the part of any who may use them. The author did not intend that they preach themselves in the hands of those who choose to use them. But if one who uses these outlines will thoroughly digest the contents of an outline before using it, it will, in a sense, become his own outline.

Brother Strong has been preaching for twenty-one years, and he has learned some things about preaching that the novice has not yet learned. Therefore much help and spiritual benefit may be derived by mastering and using the outlines herewith presented to you in this book. I know by personal experience what a book like this can mean in the hands of a young preacher. When I began preaching forty-four years ago, I did not have this help. I did not know that a book of sermon outlines was in existence.

I predict that this book will be used by a large number of young ministers. If they will use it rightly, it will prove to be of invaluable aid to them in learning to preach. Paul's admonition to Timothy was to *Preach the Word*. Those who master these outlines, following all Scripture passages indicated or implied, will be obeying Paul's injunction.

Brother Strong instructs young ministers in Central Baptist

College in the science of sermon building and delivery; through this book he may have the privilege of instructing some who may never be privileged to sit in his classes.

May the blessings of our great heavenly Father be on the writer and upon his ministry of teaching, preaching, and writing.

J. E. COBB, *Vice-President*
Central Baptist College
Conway, Arkansas

CONTENTS

Preface

Introduction

Subject Index

SUBJECT INDEX

Selected Sermon Outlines

Evangelistic

A DRAMA IN SOUL-WINNING
John 4:7

INTRODUCTION: Nowhere in the Scripture do we have a more instructive account of soul-winning than that given in this passage.

I. THE SCENE OF THE DRAMA
   A. The old well, dug by Jacob years ago, in Sychar of Samaria. (Do not despise the old.)
   B. The disciples go into the city for lunch. Jesus is tired; He sits down by the well to rest. (Work can be done while one rests.)
   C. The sinful Samaritan woman comes to draw water. (Reason from the known to the unknown.)
   D. The scene is now set for the drama in soul-winning. (It will pay to wait until the opportune time.)

II. THE STORY OF THE DRAMA
   A. The Characters
      1. The sinful Samaritan woman was deep in sin. Did she desire a better life?
      2. The seeking Saviour. Wherever there is a sinful person, there is a seeking Saviour (Luke 19:10).
   B. The Conversation
      1. Christ was tactful in His approach.
      2. He received her attention.
      3. He told her of the gift of God.
      4. Jesus spoke of her need of the Living Water.
      5. Christ tested her sincerity.
      6. The woman accepted Christ.

III. THE SEQUEL TO THE DRAMA
   A. The woman became a willing witness for Christ.
   B. Jesus did a wonderful work — On the disciple's return from lunch He said, "I have meat to eat that ye know not of."
   C. Jesus used the sequel to remind the disciples of the weight of worth — "Say not ye, there are yet four months . . . ?"

CONCLUSION: We are in a great crusade for souls. A lost world is waiting for us to come to them. Let us take to them the Living Water which satisfies.　　　D. K. B.

ESSENTIALS FOR SOUL-WINNING
Psalm 51:10-13

I. CLEANLINESS — v. 10
  - A. Creation — "create"
  - B. Renovation — "renew"
  - C. Rejuvenation

II. COMMUNION — v. 11
  - A. The presence needed — "Cast me not away."
  - B. The power realized — "Spirit"
  - C. The promise believed — "for me"

III. CONSTANCY — v. 12
  - A. Restoration — "Restore joy"
  - B. Elevation — "Uphold"
  - C. Revelation

IV. COMPASSION — v. 13
  - A. Evaluation — "transgressors"
  - B. Communication — "teach"
  - C. Conversion — "be converted"

CONCLUSION: R. M.

WHY MUST MAN BE BORN AGAIN?
John 3:7, 8

INTRODUCTION:

I. BECAUSE HE IS A SINNER, Rom. 3:23
  - A. By birth, Ps. 51:5
  - B. By nature, Eph. 2:3
  - C. By an evil heart, Jer. 17:9
  - D. By choice, John 3:19
  - E. By practice, Rom. 5:12

II. BECAUSE IT IS THE ONLY WAY INTO HEAVEN, John 3:3
  - A. Not by the law, Gal. 2:16
  - B. Not by works, Eph. 2:8
  - C. Not by moral reformation

III. BECAUSE IT PROVIDES THE ONLY ESCAPE FROM JUDGMENT, Heb. 2:3
  - A. By the everlasting birth, I Peter 1:23
  - B. By the everlasting life that ensues, I John 5:13
  - C. By the everlasting provision of the Father, Phil. 4:19

CONCLUSION: C. D. P.

THE BIRTH FROM ABOVE
John 3:1-18

INTRODUCTION:

I. THE MAN IN NEED, verses 1, 2
   - A. Religious — a Pharisee
   - B. Moral — a ruler of the Jews
   - C. Intelligent — a teacher

II. THE MAGNITUDE OF THE MATTER, verses 3-5
   - A. No seeing the kingdom without it
   - B. No entering the kingdom without it
   - C. It is imperative — "except" and "must"

III. THE MIRACULOUS NATURE
   - A. Miraculous — "from above"
   - B. It is a divine begetting — John 1:13; I John 5:1, 4
   - C. It is a spiritual quickening — Eph. 2:1
   - D. It is a new creation — II Cor. 5:17
   - E. It is the impartation of the divine nature — II Peter 1:4

IV. THE MEANS EMPLOYED FOR THE PRODUCTION, verses 5, 6
   - A. Conviction by the Holy Spirit
   - B. Proclamation of the Holy Word
     1. Hearing
     2. Repenting
     3. Believing

V. THE MYSTERY IS READILY ACKNOWLEDGED, verse 8

VI. THE MESSAGE WHICH MAKES CLEAR THE WAY, verses 14-18
   - A. The indictment — man is perishing, verse 16
   - B. The intervention of God — the gift and death of His son, verse 16
   - C. The illustration used — verse 14

VII. THE MANIFOLD BLESSINGS RECEIVED
   - A. The man was blind — now he sees
   - B. The man was condemned — now he is justified
   - C. The man was lost — now he is found
   - D. The man was perishing — now he is saved
   - E. The man was dead — now he is alive
   - F. The man was hell-bound — now he is heaven-bound
   - G. The man was an unbeliever — now he is a believer

CONCLUSION:

J. A. R.

ESSENTIALS TO REVIVAL
Ezra 7:10

INTRODUCTION:

  I. PREPARATION — "Ezra had prepared his heart"
- A. Separation — Emancipation
- B. Dedication
- C. Restoration — Consecration

  II. INVESTIGATION — "to seek the law of God"
- A. Sanctification — through the Holy Spirit
- B. Ratification — by the Holy Word
- C. Reception — through the Holy Practice — prayer

  III. PARTICIPATION — "to do it"
- A. Voluntarily
- B. Joyfully
- C. Immediately

  IV. COMMUNICATION — "to teach in Israel statutes and judgments"
- A. Proclamation — "Let the redeemed of the Lord say so."
- B. Exemplification — Teach by example

CONCLUSION:

SIX THINGS THAT THE PUBLICAN KNEW
Luke 18:9-14

INTRODUCTION:

  I. HE KNEW WHO HE WAS — a sinner

  II. HE KNEW WHERE HE WAS — afar off

  III. HE KNEW HOW HE FELT — smote upon his breast

  IV. HE KNEW WHAT HE NEEDED — mercy

  V. HE KNEW WHERE TO GET WHAT HE NEEDED — God

  VI. HE KNEW WHEN HE HAD WHAT HE NEEDED — he went down to his house

CONCLUSION:

A PRAYER FROM THE PIT
Jonah 2:1-9

I. THE DEPTH OF THE PIT, verse 1
  A. A depth of darkness
  B. A depth of degradation
  C. A depth of destruction

II. THE DANGERS OF THE PIT
  A. Encompassed by waters, verse 5
  B. Barred by the earth, verse 6
  C. Enclosed by the deep, verse 3
  D. Wrapped around by seaweeds, verse 5

III. THE DELIVERANCE FROM THE PIT
  A. A manifestation of grace — "divinely wrought"
  B. A revelation of greatness — "highly benevolent"
  C. A proclamation of growth — "Jonah, the most unlikely"

IV. THE DELIVERER PRAISED
  A. For the salvation of life
  B. By the sacrifice of thanksgiving
  C. By a solemn vow

CONCLUSION: H. O. P.

THE PRODIGAL SON
Luke 15:11-24

INTRODUCTION:

I. THE PRODIGAL AT HOME
  A. Inheritance demanded, v. 12
  B. Incited division, v. 12
  C. Independence desired, v. 13

II. THE PRODIGAL AWAY FROM HOME
  A. Incurred disgrace, v. 13
  B. Increased debauchery, vv. 14-16
  C. Inclined toward degradation

III. THE PRODIGAL RETURNING HOME
  A. Intelligent deduction, v. 17
  B. Increasing desire
  C. Inverted decision, v. 18

IV. THE PRODIGAL AT HOME AGAIN
  A. Immediate designation — "my son"
  B. Intimate devotion, vv. 20-22
  C. Instant delight, vv. 23, 24

CONCLUSION: O. L. M.

17

BARABBAS
Mark 15:1-15

INTRODUCTION:
1. Barabbas is usually despised
2. Barabbas is a representative sinner

I. THE SINS OF BARABBAS
A. "A notable prisoner," Matt. 27:16
B. An insurgent, Mark 15:7
C. A robber, John 18:40
D. A murderer, Luke 23:19
(All of these things can be said of any sinner.)

II. THE STATE OF BARABBAS
A. He was guilty, Rom. 3:19
B. He was condemned, John 3:18
C. He was bound, Rom. 5:6
D. He was without hope, Eph. 2:12
E. He was under sentence of death, Rom. 6:23
(All of these things could be said of any sinner.)

III. THE SUBSTITUTE FOR BARABBAS
A. An undeserved substitute, Rom. 5:10; II Cor. 5:21
B. An unexpected release, Matt. 27:26; John 11:44
C. An unhampered freedom, John 8:36; Gal. 5:1
(All of these things can be said of any sinner who is substituted for by Christ.)

CONCLUSION:

C. H. S.

WHAT SHALL I DO WITH JESUS?
Matthew 27:19-23

INTRODUCTION:

I. CONSIDER THE PERSON OF YOUR CHOICE
   A. He is the Son of God —
      1. Proclaimed by God's prophets, Acts 10:43
      2. Announced by God's angels, Luke 2:8-14
      3. Approved by heaven, Matt. 3:17
      4. Acknowledged by hell
   B. He is the Son of Man —
      1. Manifested by His life
      2. Declared by His Word
      3. Proclaimed by His works
      4. Testified by His influence
      5. Proved by His resurrection
   C. He is your Saviour, Isa. 53:5, 6
   D. He is your Sovereign, Acts 2:36

II. CONSIDER YOUR POSITION IN THE CHOICE TO BE MADE
    What must I do with Jesus?
    A. Accept or reject Him — personal accountability, Rom. 14:12
    B. Let Him in your heart or shut Him out — an attempted evasion, Rev. 3:20
    C. Confess or deny Him, Matt. 10:32, 33
    D. Take your stand for Him or against Him, Matt. 12:30

III. CONSIDER THE PROMISE OF YOUR CHOICE
    A. Your acceptance or rejection before God, John 3:18
    B. Your becoming a son of God or remaining a child of the devil, John 1:12
    C. Your peace within or conflict without, Rom. 5:1
    D. Your joy or unhappiness forever, I Peter 1:8
    E. Eternal life or the Second Death, John 3:26

CONCLUSION:

A PRAYER OF A SINNER
Luke 18:13

INTRODUCTION:

I. IT WAS TO THE RIGHT SOURCE: "GOD."
   - A. Against God he had sinned
   - B. Only God can forgive sin
   - C. God sees sin

II. IT WAS IN THE RIGHT SPIRIT: "STANDING AFAR OFF."
   - A. Humility — (Recognized his state)
   - B. Repentant — (Forgiveness)
   - C. Received his portion

III. IT WAS FOR THE RIGHT SUBSTANCE: "BE MERCIFUL."
   - A. Not justice
   - B. Recognized limitation of his own power
   - C. Feared God's wrath

IV. IT WAS BY THE RIGHT SUBJECTS: "TO ME A SINNER."
   - A. A condemned sinner
   - B. A dying sinner
   - C. A burdened sinner
   - D. A sinner unmindful of hypocrites
   - E. A saved sinner

CONCLUSION:

WILT THOU BE MADE WHOLE?
John 5:1-9

INTRODUCTION:

I. THEN YOU MUST KNOW THAT SOMETHING IS WRONG WITH YOU
   A. Impotent
   B. Blind
   C. Halt
   D. Withered
   E. Diseased

II. THEN YOU MUST WANT SOMETHING DONE ABOUT IT
   A. Immediately
   B. Completely
   C. Personally

III. THEN YOU MUST KNOW THAT YOU CANNOT HEAL YOURSELF
   A. Not by moral reformation
   B. Not by education
   C. Not by legislation
   D. Not by religious participation

IV. THEN YOU MUST APPEAL TO THE GREAT PHYSICIAN
   A. Come by faith
   B. Call upon Him
   C. Repent of your sin
   D. Accept His remedy

CONCLUSION:
   "Go away whole."

THE GREAT PHYSICIAN
Isaiah 1:5, 6; Matthew 9:10-13

INTRODUCTION:

I. WHY MAN NEEDS A PHYSICIAN
   A. The heart is faint, Isa. 1:5
   B. The head is sick, Isa. 1:6
   C. The tongue is still, Rom. 3:19
   D. The eyes are blind, II Cor. 4:3, 4
   E. The ears are stopped, Acts 7:51, 57

II. MAN CANNOT HEAL HIMSELF
   A. No man trusts his own remedy when he is really sick
   B. Works and law are insufficient
   C. Some will delay to call the physician
   D. Here, sometimes the "Doctor's Out"
   E. Medical Science vs. Christ

III. JESUS IS THE GREAT PHYSICIAN
   A. He loves His patients
   B. He has all knowledge
   C. He has all power
   D. His cure is certain
   E. His terms are easy
   F. He respects all alike, Isa. 55:1

IV. HIS CURE IS LAID OUT!
   A. His Word, Heb. 4:12; Ps. 107:20
   B. His Spirit, John 16:7-11
   C. His Blood, Heb. 9:14

CONCLUSION:

   Call on the Great Physician, Jer. 8:22

THE RICH FOOL
Luke 12:16-21

INTRODUCTION:

I. THE RICH MAN'S POSSESSIONS, verse 16
   A. Plentiful
   B. Powerful — (influential)
   C. Perishable

II. THE RICH MAN'S PERPLEXITIES, verse 17
   A. Proportionate to the amount of goods
   B. Proprietor versus steward
   C. Pace of the increase

III. THE RICH MAN'S PROCLAMATION, verse 18
   A. He resolves on the means of accumulation
   B. He forms his arrangements
   C. He reckons on his riches as the joy and portion of his soul
   D. He confidently calculates on an extended existence, verse 19

IV. THE RICH MAN'S SUDDEN AND FATAL PRONOUNCEMENT
   A. He is disturbed by the voice of Deity
   B. The sudden termination of his career
   C. The eternal ruin of his soul

CONCLUSION:

H. O. P.

A SAD FUNERAL
Ecclesiastes 8:1-11

INTRODUCTION:

I. A SOLEMN SIGHT — "a burial"
- A. Buried *to* and not *with* Christ
- B. Buried *in* and not *from* sin
- C. Buried *by* unbelief and not *in* faith

II. A SOLEMN REFLECTION — "I saw the wicked buried."
- A. Seen by wicked friends
- B. Seen by wicked foes
- C. Seen by wicked forces

III. A SOLEMN WARNING — "I saw the wicked buried who had come and gone from the place of the holy."
- A. They had come for reformation and gone without regeneration
- B. They had come for profession and gone without possession
- C. They had come for religion and gone without redemption
- D. They had come for instruction and gone without illumination

CONCLUSION:

H. O. P.

PEOPLE AND PASSIONS
Luke 18:35-43

INTRODUCTION:
  I. THE MAN
    A. Conscious of his need
    B. Concerned about his condition
    C. Called for help
      1. He called for the right thing
      2. He called at the right time
      3. He called unto the right person
  II. THE MULTITUDE
    A. Revealed the plan of Satan
    B. Manifested the proof of selfishness
    C. Demonstrated the power of sin
  III. THE MASTER
    A. Had compassion — He moved to meet the man's need
    B. Had correction — He met the man's need
    C. Had completeness — The man was made whole
      1. Inwardly
      2. Immediately

CONCLUSION:
      1. The man followed Jesus
      2. The man glorified God
      3. The people praised God

A. D. L.

25

THE MAN CHRIST SENT HOME
Luke 8:26-39

INTRODUCTION:
- A. The condition of the community
- B. The choice of the crowd
- C. The channel of the conquest

I. THE MAN'S CONDITION
- A. He was unclean, v. 27
- B. He was unclothed, v. 27
- C. He was unbalanced, v. 27
  1. Lived among tombs
  2. Refused to be tamed
  3. Abused himself (Mark 4:4, 5)

II. THE MAN'S CURE
- A. A releasing change
- B. A recognized change
  1. By the delivered (instantaneous devotion)
  2. By others
     a. Sitting at the feet
     b. Clothed
     c. In his right mind
- C. A renowned change (famous or published change), v. 36

III. THE MAN'S COMMISSION — "Go home to thy friends"
- A. A specified place
- B. A selected message
- C. A surrendered life

CONCLUSION:
- A. What if Jesus had not come this way?
- B. What if this man had refused to accept Jesus?
- C. Does your life need Jesus?

A. R. R.

THE DYING SINNER'S DEATH TO SIN
Luke 23:39-45

INTRODUCTION:

I. HIS CONDEMNATION, v. 40
   A. His guilt, Isa. 53:6; Rom. 3:23
   B. His confession, Luke 5:8
   C. His dying, Rom. 5:12
      1. Near death, I Sam. 20:3
      2. Bound — helpless, Eph. 2:8, 9; John 10:9; Acts 4:12, John 14:6

II. HIS APPLICATION, v. 42
   A. Personal — *me*
   B. His belief, Mark 9:24
   C. His appeal, Luke 18:13

III. HIS SALVATION, v. 43
   A. He was saved, Acts 16:31
      1. From sin
      2. From self
      3. From Satan
   B. He was assured, Mark 2:5
   C. For fellowship

CONCLUSION:

THE MASTER COMES AND CALLS
John 11:28

INTRODUCTION:

I. HE CALLS TO SALVATION
- A. A salvation that separates
  1. Abram, Gen. 12:1
  2. Israel, Ex. 3:16, 17
  3. The promise, II Cor. 6:17, 18
- B. A salvation that satisfies
  1. Thirst, John 7:37
  2. Hunger, John 6:50, 51
  3. Anxiety, Rev. 22:17
     a. Sins are forgiven, I John 2:12
     b. We are children of God, Gal. 3:26
     c. We shall never perish, John 10:28, 29
- C. A salvation that secures
  1. By Holy Spirit, Eph. 1:13
  2. Through His Word, I John 5:12, 13
  3. From judgment, John 5:24

II. THE MASTER CALLS TO ASSOCIATION
- A. In the name of Jesus, Matt. 18:20
- B. With the Father and Son, I John 1:3
- C. With other believers, Acts 2:42

III. THE MASTER CALLS TO DEDICATION
- A. To a life of service, I Cor. 10:31
- B. To a life of sacrifice, Acts 1:8

IV. THE MASTER CALLS TO EXPECTATION
- A. Because of our hope
- B. Because of our home, John 14:1-3; I Peter 1:4; I Thess. 4:13-18

CONCLUSION:

28

THIS YEAR ALSO
Luke 13:6-9

INTRODUCTION:

I. SUGGESTS A RETROSPECT — "These three years I come seeking fruit"
  A. The planting — "had planted"
  B. The position — "in his vineyard"
  C. The planning — "fruit"
  D. The procrastination — "three years"

II. SETS FORTH A JUDGMENT — "Cut it down"
  A. The profession — "a fig tree"
  B. The perplexity — "cumbereth the ground"

III. DISPLAYS A FAVOR — "Let it alone this year also"
  A. The pity of the dresser
  B. The promise of the year

IV. SIGNIFIES A NEED — "Dig about it and dung it"
  A. Piercing and prodding — "dig about it"
  B. Provision — "dung it"

V. REVEALS A DESIRE — "Bring forth fruit"
  A. The potential is there
  B. The profit is desirable

VI. IMPLIES A LIMIT — "Then after that"
  A. The person — "thou"
  B. The providence — "shalt"
  C. The power — "cut down"

CONCLUSION:

R. S. B.

THE LOST SHEEP
Luke 15:1-6

INTRODUCTION:

I. THE SHEPHERD'S DISCOVERY, v. 4 — "A lost sheep"
The lost is:
A. Lonely
B. Outside
C. Sinful
D. Tempted   (J. D. B.)

II. THE SAVIOUR'S DECISION, v. 4 — "Go after that which is lost"
A. Through the preaching of the Gospel
B. Through the conviction of the Holy Spirit
C. Through the prayers of His people

III. THE SEARCHER'S DILIGENCE, v. 4 — "Until he find it"
Until he finds it:
A. The Saviour's heart is grieved
B. The fellowship is destroyed
C. The sheep's usefulness is voided

IV. THE STRONG DELIVERER, v. 5 — "He layeth it on his shoulders"
On his shoulders:
A. Lifted out of the pitfall
B. Laid above the powers about it
C. To live for the person of Christ

V. THE SAINTS' DELIGHT, v. 6 — "Rejoice with me"
A. Rejoice in the finding
B. Rejoice over the found
C. Rejoice in the new fate

CONCLUSION:

O. L. M.

CHRIST AS THE DOOR
John 10:9

INTRODUCTION:

I. THE DOOR TO SALVATION — "We shall be saved"
   A. Saved from something:
      1. Sin
      2. Satan
      3. Self
      4. Separation
   B. Saved with something:
      1. Sacrifice
      2. Substitution
   C. Saved to something:
      1. Fellowship
      2. Followship

II. THE DOOR TO SECURITY — "We shall go in"
   A. Secured by His promise
   B. Secured by His presence
   C. Secured by His power

III. THE DOOR TO SERVICE — "We shall go out"
   A. To learn — we are His disciples
   B. To live — we are His people
   C. To lead — we are His agents

IV. THE DOOR TO SATISFACTION — "We shall find pasture"
   A. A pleasant and peaceful pasture
   B. A plenteous pasture

CONCLUSION:

W. R.

THE EXPERIENCES OF A SLAVE
I Samuel 30:11-19

INTRODUCTION (Setting)

    A. Ziklag had been burned while David and the armies of Israel fought against the Philistines

    B. David inquired of the Lord and pursued the Amalekites — an Egyptian was found

        1. "to whom belongest thou?"

        2. "whence art thou?"

            a. All men belong to someone, Rom. 6:16; John 8:34

            b. Egypt — a type of the flesh

  I. HE WAS FORSAKEN, v. 13 — "My master left me because . . . I fell sick"

    A. He was left without his health

    B. He was left without help (as far as others to help)

    C. He was left helpless (as far as helping himself)

 II. HE WAS FAMISHED, v. 12 — "Had eaten no bread"

    A. Unsaved men are now hungry

    B. The world does not give or leave that which will satisfy

    C. Starvation will ensue unless one is found in time

III. HE WAS FOUND, v. 11 — "Found an Egyptian in the field"

    A. He did not find himself — he was found of another

    B. The sinner will not find himself — he must be found of another

        1. Calling

        2. Convicting

        3. Converting

IV. HE WAS FED, v. 11 — "Gave him bread . . . and water"

    A. The Bread of Life is needed

    B. The Water of Life is needed

    (His old master had left him nothing — The new master gave him all he needed.)

 V. HE WAS FREED, v. 15

    A. He refused to return to the service of his old master

    B. He voluntarily entered David's army

CONCLUSION:

H. O. P.

1/28/79 AM

FROM "GIVE ME" TO "MAKE ME"
Luke 15:11-24

INTRODUCTION:

I. THE "GIVE ME" LIFE, v. 12
- A. How the "give me" life began
    1. He assumed complete control of a quantity of goods, v. 13a
    2. He chose an environment to suit his desires, v. 13b
    3. He spent all for his own pleasure, v. 13c
- B. How the "give me" life terminated
    1. It terminated in personal destitution, v. 14
    2. It forced him into undesirable employment, v. 15
    3. It brought him to hunger, v. 16

II. THE "MAKE ME" LIFE, vv. 18, 19
- A. How the "make me" life began
    1. With a recognition of his own sin against God and man, v. 18
    2. With a willingness to accept the status of a servant
    3. With a journey in the reverse direction, v. 20a
- B. How the "make me" life terminated
    1. Restoration and forgiveness, v. 20b
    2. Food and clothing furnished, vv. 22, 23a
    3. He found the true joy of living, v. 24b

CONCLUSION:

G. A. P. P.

THE PRODIGAL SON
Luke 15:11-24

INTRODUCTION:

I. GOING AWAY FROM HOME
   A. Restless and rebellious
   B. Roving
   C. Riotous
   D. Reckless
   E. Ruined

II. COMING BACK HOME
   A. Reflecting
   B. Reasoning
   C. Resolving
   D. Returning

III. HOME AGAIN FOREVER
   A. Recognized
   B. Received
   C. Robed
   D. Ringed
   E. Rejoicing

CONCLUSION:

THE PRODIGAL SON
Luke 15:11-24

INTRODUCTION:

I. HIS REALIZATION, v. 17
   - A. The failure of materialism
   - B. The failure of his chosen environment
   - C. The failure of employment
   - D. The fault of personal pleasure

II. HIS READINESS, v. 18a
   - A. His recognition of God
   - B. His recognition of man
   - C. His recognition of the status of a servant
   - D. His reversal of directions

III. HIS REMORSE, vv. 18b, 19, 21
   - A. Sin against heaven
   - B. Sin against his father
   - C. Sin against himself
   - D. Sin against society

IV. HIS REWARD, vv. 22, 23
   - A. Recognized by his father
   - B. Received by the father
   - C. Robed by the father
   - D. Ringed by the father
   - E. Restored by the father
     1. True food found
     2. True pleasure in living
     3. Shod for service

CONCLUSION:

V. B. B.

35

THE PRODIGAL SON
Luke 15:11-24

INTRODUCTION:

I. THE RAMPAGE OF AN URGE
   A. Caused by allurement
   B. Encouraged by insistence
   C. Supported by premeditation

II. THE ROAD OF THE WAYWARD
   A. Easy to enter
   B. Difficult to desert
   C. Certain of failure

III. THE REMORSE OF THE WANDERER
   A. Out of funds and without counsel
   B. Out of food and without comfort
   C. Out of fellowship and without companions

IV. THE RETURN OF THE PENITENT
   A. Memory opened a door
   B. Humility was permitted to develop
   C. Determination took control

CONCLUSION:

S. F. L.

36

WHAT SHALL I DO?
Mark 10:17

INTRODUCTION:

I. LOOK UNTO ME FOR REVELATION, (Isa. 45:22)
   A. The revelation of a person
   B. The revelation of a power
   C. The revelation of a passion

II. COME UNTO ME FOR SALVATION, (Matt. 11:28)
   A. Salvation from sin
   B. Salvation from self
   C. Salvation from Satan
   D. Salvation for service

III. LEARN OF ME FOR INSTRUCTION, (Matt. 11:29)
   A. Learn to live
   B. Learn to love
   C. Learn to lead

IV. FOLLOW THOU ME FOR CONSECRATION, (John 21:22)
   A. Follow Me in sacrificing
   B. Follow Me in suffering
   C. Follow Me in serving

V. ABIDE IN ME FOR ASSOCIATION, (John 15:4)
   A. Abide in My presence
   B. Abide in My passion
   C. Abide in My promise

VI. TURN YE UNTO ME FOR TRANSFORMATION, (Zech. 1:3)
   A. Turn from degradation to regeneration
   B. Turn from condemnation to justification
   C. Turn from desecration to sanctification

CONCLUSION:

G. F. V.

SON, REMEMBER
Luke 16:19-31
Text: verse 25

INTRODUCTION:

I. REMEMBER WHERE HELL IS:
    A. Away from God's presence, Matt. 25:41
    B. At the end of a misspent life
    C. At the end of the broad way, Matt. 7:13, 14

II. REMEMBER WHAT HELL IS:
    A. It is a place:
        1. Of darkness, II Peter 2:4
        2. Of unsatisfied desires:
            a. Cry for mercy
            b. Send Lazarus
            c. Send Lazarus to my brethren
    B. It is a state:
        1. Of intensive pain
        2. Of separation
        3. Of dreadful monotony
    C. It is a definite tenure:
        1. Not like the animals
        2. Not just the grave
        3. Not a sudden consuming

III. REMEMBER WHO WILL BE IN HELL:
    A. Wicked and ungodly, Ps. 9:17
    B. Degraded society, Rev. 22:15
    C. All unbelievers, Rev. 20:15

IV. REMEMBER WHY THERE IS A HELL:
    A. Because of sin
    B. God owes it to punish sin
    C. God owes it to separate saints and sinners in eternity

V. REMEMBER HOW YOU COULD HAVE ESCAPED HELL:
    A. By hearing the Gospel
    B. By repenting of sin
    C. By exercising faith in Christ

CONCLUSION:

THE LAST NIGHT IN TOWN
Genesis 19:12-16; 24-29

INTRODUCTION:

I. A NIGHT OF WOE, v. 13
   A. Because of wickedness, 13:13
   B. Because of worldliness
   C. Because of the weakness in yielding to sin

II. A NIGHT OF WARNING, v. 14
   A. He walked
   B. He warned
   C. He witnessed
   D. His efforts were worthless

III. A NIGHT OF WONDER
   A. About his people
   B. About his past
   C. About his practices

IV. A NIGHT OF WITHERED HOPE, vv. 15, 16
   A. He watched and worried
   B. He worshiped and wept
   C. He waited and withdrew

V. A NIGHT OF WAGES
   A. He lost his wife
   B. He lost his wealth
   C. He lost his life's work

CONCLUSION:

   1. God is warning you now — prepare for destruction.
   2. God is calling you now — get out of Sodom.
   3. God is inviting you now.
   4. God's people are praying for you now.

G. E. H.

Doctrinal

SALVATION
Titus 2:11-15

INTRODUCTION: THREE THEORIES
    1. By works
    2. By grace and works
    3. By grace (Eph. 2:8-10)

I. THE NEED OF SALVATION (Rom. 3:23; Isa. 53:6)
Man is a sinner:
    A. By birth and nature, Ps. 51:5
    B. By choice, John 3:19
    C. By practice, Rom. 5:12

II. THE SOURCE OF SALVATION
    A. Not in materialism
    B. Not by symbols
        1. Baptism — the fact of salvation
        2. Lord's Supper — the source of salvation
    C. In Christ (Acts 4:12; John 3:18; I John 5:12; John 3:16)

III. THE STEPS IN SALVATION
    A. Repentance
    B. Faith (Acts 20:21)

IV. THE ASSURANCE OF SALVATION (John 3:18; II Tim. 1:12)
    A. The Word of God
    B. The witness of the Spirit
    C. The sense of forgiveness (Rom. 5:1)

CONCLUSION: Acts 16:31; 5:31

THE DIVINE PATTERN OF BAPTISM
Matthew 3:13-17

INTRODUCTION:

I. As to the Subject (Person)
   A. As portrayed by Jesus
   B. As shown by John's demanding fruits of repentance, Matt. 3:8; John 15:5

II. As to the Design (Purpose)
   A. To manifest sonship, John 1:31; Acts 10:47; Rom. 8:14-17
   B. To picture faith in the death, burial, and resurrection of Christ
   C. To proclaim one's death to sin and resurrection to a new life, Rom. 6:4, 5

III. As to the Mode (Pattern)
   A. As shown by the meaning of "baptize" — to dip, immerse, submerge, plunge
   B. As shown by the baptism of Jesus, Matt. 3:16
   C. As shown by other inspired examples, John 3:23; Acts 8:38

IV. As to the Authority (Power)
   A. It is of heavenly origin, Matt. 21:25
   B. It was vested in John the Baptist
   C. It was included in the church's commission, Matt. 28:18-20
   D. It was Christian from the beginning
      1. Received by Christ and His disciples
      2. Belonged to the gospel dispensation, Mark 1:1-4

V. As to the Administrator (Propriety)
   A. One sent from God, John 1:6
   B. One clothed with right authority, I Cor. 3:21-23; Matt. 28:18-20

CONCLUSION:

D. N. J.

THE MESSAGE OF THE LORD'S SUPPER
Matthew 26:17-35

INTRODUCTION:

I. THE HISTORICAL MESSAGE
   A. A message of the ruin of sin, Rom. 3:23; 5:12; Isa. 53:6
   B. A message of the remedy for sin, Heb. 9:22; I Peter 1: 18, 19
   C. A message that we have died with Christ (we have been identified with Him in His death)

II. THE PROPHETIC MESSAGE, I Cor. 11:25, 26
   A. Emphasizes the first coming of Christ
   B. Prophesies the second coming of Christ
   C. Preserves the doctrine of Christ's coming

III. THE PRACTICAL MESSAGE
   A. A message of self-examination
   B. A message of humility
   C. A message of deep spirituality
   D. A message that motivates gratitude

CONCLUSION:

A. R. R.

THE MESSAGE OF THE LORD'S SUPPER
I Corinthians 11:23-34

INTRODUCTION:

    1. "What mean ye by these stones?" Josh. 4:6, 21

    2. The message of the ordinance

I. A MESSAGE OF RUIN, II Cor. 5:14

    A. His death reflects our ruin

    B. The scope of death, Rom. 5:12

    C. The avenue affected, Isa. 1:5, 6

II. A MESSAGE OF REDEMPTION

    A. Redemption by price — payment

    B. Redemption by power — blood

    C. Redemption by person — Christ, Gal. 3:13

III. A MESSAGE OF REAL FELLOWSHIP

    A. Kindred experiences, Acts 2:40

    B. Doctrinal fellowship

    C. Fraternal relationship — one church

IV. A MESSAGE OF HIS RETURN

    A. The aspects of the lesson

    B. Importance of His teaching

    C. Completed victory

CONCLUSION: Make the proper examination.

THE BELIEVER'S NEED OF THE LORD'S SUPPER
I Corinthians 11:23-29

INTRODUCTION:

I. As CONFESSION OF CHRIST
   A. His death for our salvation
   B. His deliverance for our justification
   C. His departure for our glorification

II. As COMMUNION WITH CHRIST
   A. With the person of Christ
   B. With the power of Christ
   C. With the promise of Christ

III. As CONSECRATION TO CHRIST
   A. Requires examination
   B. Suggests sanctification
   C. Maintains revelation

IV. As COMMEMORATION OF CHRIST
   A. His crucifixion
   B. His resurrection
   C. His proclamation to return

CONCLUSION:

R. A.

THE LORD'S SUPPER
I Corinthians 11:23, 24

Introduction:

I. A Commemoration — "In remembrance of me"
   A. Of His spotless life
   B. Of His changeless love
   C. Of His ceaseless loyalty

II. A Communion — "Eat it with me"
   A. The association of His presence
   B. The evaluation of His power
   C. The realization of His promise

III. A Confession — "For the remission of sin"
   A. The need for salvation
   B. The need for sanctification
   C. The need for preservation

IV. A Consecration — "Till I come"
   A. Continue the search for the groping sinner
   B. Continue your study for a growth in grace
   C. Continue your service for a growing church

V. A Covenant — "Blood of the covenant"
   A. The last will
   B. The living way
   C. The leading writ

Conclusion:

J. O. D.

45

THE SUPREMACY OF THE CHURCH
Matthew 16:18

INTRODUCTION:

 I. HER ORIGIN — the grandest, Eph. 3:9-11
 II. HER ORGANIZATION
    A. Her Architect — the greatest, Eph. 2:21
    B. Her Builder — the wisest, Matt. 16:18
    C. Her Foundation — the surest, I Peter 2:4-6
 III. HER ORDER
    A. Her Head — the highest, Eph. 1:22
    B. Her unity — the strongest, Eph. 4:4
    C. Her worship — the purest, I Peter 2:5
    D. Her praises — the sweetest, Heb. 2:12, 13, 15
 IV. HER OUTLOOK
    Her destiny — the noblest, Eph. 5:27

CONCLUSION:

THE RELATION OF CHRIST AND THE CHURCH
Ephesians 5:21-33

INTRODUCTION:

I. THE RELATIONSHIP OF CHRIST TO THE CHURCH
   A. He is her Love, v. 25
   B. He is her Redeemer, v. 25
   C. He is her Husband, v. 23
      1. He is her authority
      2. She is His responsibility
   D. He is her Sanctifier, v. 26
   E. He is her Satisfier, v. 29
      1. He nourishes her with His Word
      2. He embraces her with His arms of love
      3. He comforts her with His Spirit
   F. He is her awaiting Bridegroom, v. 27

II. THE RELATIONSHIP OF THE CHURCH TO CHRIST. It is that of:
   A. Saved ones, v. 23
   B. Members of His body, Rom. 12:5
   C. Submission, v. 24
   D. Reverence, v. 33

CONCLUSIONS:

THIS MINISTRY
II Corinthians 3:1-18; 4:1-6

INTRODUCTION: THE TRUE MINISTER'S CREDENTIALS
1. Called by God the Father, Gal. 1:15
2. Commissioned by God the Son, Acts 26:16
3. Clothed by God the Spirit, Acts 9:17
4. Certified by the Church, Acts 13:2

I. THIS MINISTRY RECEIVED
   A. Preach the precepts, II Tim. 4:1-3
   B. Preach to profit, II Tim. 2:14
   C. Preach without partiality, I Tim. 5:1
   D. Practice what you preach, I Tim. 6:13, 14

II. THIS MINISTRY REVEALED
    A. One of problems, II Cor. 11:23-27; 12:7
    B. One of purpose, II Tim. 2:10
    C. One of passion, Rom. 9:3
    D. One of prayer, Rom. 10:1
    E. One of power, Acts 9:17

III. THIS MINISTRY REWARDED
     A. Difficult but delightful, Col. 1:24
     B. Dispensational, Col. 1:25
     C. Deep, Col. 1:26, 27
     D. Developing, Col. 1:28
     E. Dynamic, Col. 1:29

CONCLUSIONS:

THE CHURCH
Matthew 16:13-20

INTRODUCTION:

I. HER MARVELOUS CHARACTER
   A. She is a distinct body (I Cor. 10:32)
   B. She is of His making (Matt. 16:18; Isa. 28:16)
   C. She is called out for His own name (Isa. 43:21)
   D. She is filled with His fullness (Eph. 1:22, 23; 4:15)

II. HER PRESENT PRIVILEGES
   A. She occupies (Luke 19:12-15; II Cor. 5:20)
   B. She suffers for Him (I Peter 2:20, 21; 4:14-16)
   C. She is a co-worker with Him (II Cor. 6:1; I Cor. 3:9)

III. HER FUTURE PROSPECTS
   A. She looks for Him (Acts 1:11; I Thess. 1:10)
   B. She expects to be caught up by Him (I Thess. 4:16)
   C. She expects to be made like Him (Phil. 3:20, 21)
   D. She expects to be married to Him (Rev. 19:7; Gen. 24)
   E. She expects to reign with Him (Rev. 20:6; I Cor. 6:2; Rev. 5:10)

CONCLUSION:

THE GRACE OF GIVING
II Corinthians 8:1-16, text v. 7

INTRODUCTION:

I. PROMPTING GRACE, v. 5
  - A. Not law — "willing of themselves"
  - B. Not material — "gave their own selves"
  - C. God's will — "by the will of God"

II. POWERFUL GRACE, v. 3
  - A. "For their power"
  - B. "Beyond their power"
  - C. "Praying us"

III. PROVING GRACE, v. 8
  - A. "Not by commandment"
  - B. Prove who you are
  - C. Prove what you are

IV. PERFORMING GRACE, v. 11
  - A. "A readiness of will"
  - B. "There may be a performance"
  - C. "Doers not hearers only"

V. PROPORTIONING GRACE, v. 14
  - A. "By an equality"
  - B. God is an equalizer
  - C. Commend Titus to continue

CONCLUSION:

THE GRACE OF GIVING
II Corinthians 8:1-24

Introduction:
1. The lesson background
2. The need for this instruction today
3. The measure of a man

I. The Prompting of Giving
   A. The urge of example — Christ, v. 9
   B. The urge of experience — inward, v. 3-6
   C. The urge of expediency, v. 10

II. The Portion of Giving
   A. A liberal portion, v. 3
   B. A willing portion, v. 12
   C. An equal portion, vv. 12-14

III. The Purpose of Giving
   A. The supplying of kingdom needs
   B. The proving of our love, vv. 8, 24
   C. The proving of our growth, vv. 6, 7

IV. The Pay of Giving
   A. A satisfied conscience
   B. A supplied church
   C. A special crown

Conclusion:

A. R. R.

THE GOSPEL —

1. of God, I Thess. 2:9
2. of Grace, Acts 20:24
3. of Christ, Rom. 15:19
4. of the Kingdom, Mark 1:14

INTRODUCTION:

I. ITS ATTRIBUTES ARE UNIQUE, Col. 1:15
  A. Indicates a favor, John 3:16
  B. Indicates a freedom, Rom. 6:23b
  C. Indicates a force, Rom. 1:16

II. ITS APPLICATION IS UNIVERSAL, II Peter 3:9
  A. Indicates fruition, II Sam. 7:16
  B. Indicates fellowship, II Cor. 4:3; 8:4
  C. Indicates finality, Rev. 14:6, 7

III. ITS APPEAL IS URGENT, Mark 13:10
  A. Indicates falsity, Gal. 1:8
  B. Indicates folly
  C. Indicates futility

CONCLUSION:

1. The inference — other than ordained
2. Indictment — "Let him be accursed"

S. F. L.

Ethical

A PRAYING CHURCH
Acts 1:1-14

I. A Praying Church Is a STAYING Church
  A. Her members stay in the service (in place)
  B. Her members stay in line (in the will of God)
  C. Her members stay in the faith

II. A Praying Church Is a SWAYING Church
  A. Her members sway each other (fellowship)
  B. Her members sway God (prayer)
  C. Her members sway the world (influence)

III. A Praying Church Is a PAYING Church
  A. Her members pay with the right motive
  B. Her members pay at the right time
  C. Her members pay the right amount

IV. A Praying Church Is an OBEYING Church
  A. As to doctrine
  B. As to practice
  C. As to commission

Conclusion:
  Are you a *praying, swaying, paying, obeying* member?

z. w. s.

53

WHY I SHOULD NOT FEAR
Isaiah 41:1-10

INTRODUCTION:

I. PERSONAL POSSESSION — "I am thy God"
   A. Omniscience
   B. Omnipotence
   C. Omnipresence

II. PERSONAL PRESENCE — "I am with thee"
   A. The best company
   B. The greatest commander
   C. The richest comfort

III. PERSONAL PROMISE — "I will strengthen thee"
   A. For a noble work
   B. Against life's woes
   C. For individual worth

IV. PERSONAL PROVISION — "I will help thee"
   A. In the time of trouble
   B. In the time of triumph
   C. To overcome temptation

V. PERSONAL PROTECTION — "I will uphold thee"
   A. From the degradation of sin
   B. From the defilement of self
   C. From the allurement of Satan

CONCLUSION:

CHRIST AND THE BELIEVER
Colossians 3:1-4

INTRODUCTION:

I. SALVATION — "risen with Christ"
   A. Risen from death
   B. Risen above debt
   C. Risen to dedication

II. RESIGNATION — "affection on things above"
   A. Resigned to love
   B. Resigned to learn
   C. Resigned to live

III. EXPECTATION — "Hid with Christ"
   A. Expect elevation
   B. Expect sanctification
   C. Expect glorification

IV. REALIZATION — "When . . . Christ shall appear"
   A. The plan of creation
   B. The purpose of regeneration
   C. The power of the resurrection

CONCLUSION:

THE BIBLE AS A MIRROR
James 1:1-27

INTRODUCTION: A mirror reflects the true character of things. So the Bible is a mirror of both man and God, sin and holiness, earth and heaven.

I. THE BIBLE REFLECTS THE TRUE CHARACTER OF MAN:
   A. His heart (Jer. 17:9; Matt. 15:19)
   B. His mind (Rom. 8:7)
   C. His hope (Eph. 2:12)

II. THE BIBLE REFLECTS THE GREAT LOVE OF GOD:
   A. His general love (John 3:16)
   B. His special love (Eph. 5:25)
   C. His personal love (Gal. 2:20)
   D. His undying love (Jer. 31:3)

III. THE BIBLE REFLECTS THE GRACE AND GLORY OF JESUS CHRIST:
   A. His spotless character (I Peter 1:19)
   B. His perfect work (Heb. 10:12-14)
   C. His personal glory (John 17:5)
   D. His saving power (Heb. 7:25)

CONCLUSION:

C. E.

THREE GREAT THINGS
Revelation 1:5, 6

INTRODUCTION:
- I. A GREAT AFFECTION — "He loved us."
  - A. Because of creation
  - B. Because of regeneration
  - C. Because of sanctification
  - D. Because of glorification
- II. A GREAT PURIFICATION — "He washed us."
  - A. From something — "our sin"
  - B. In something — "sinless blood"
  - C. For something — "service"
- III. A GREAT TRANSFORMATION — "He made us."
  - A. His kindred — "sons"
    (From aliens to sons)
  - B. Kind — "priests"
    (From unbelievers to priests)
  - C. "Kings"
    (From subjects of Satan to kings of God)

CONCLUSION:

DISCIPLES IN THREE DIMENSIONS

INTRODUCTION:
- I. DEMAS — "Loved this present world," II Tim. 4:10
  - A. Of escape and ease (Romanticism)
  - B. Of limited vision and understanding (Epicureanism — pleasure)
  - C. Of Godless materialism
- II. DIOTREPHES — "loved the preeminence among the brethren," III John 9
  - A. Position and prestige
  - B. Promise and provision
  - C. Power and persuasion
- III. DEMETRIUS — "hath a good report," III John 12
  - A. Of all men — without
  - B. Of the truth — within
  - C. Of contemporaries — besides

CONCLUSION: R. B. C.

FIVE WELLS

I. A WELL OF FOUNDATION (Gen. 16:7)
   A. Located in the wilderness
   B. Located by the fountain
   C. Where God was found (Gen. 16:13, 14)

II. A WELL OF SALVATION (Gen. 21:19)
   A. Her eyes were opened to the well (John 6:44)
   B. She saw the well
      1. A well of revelation (Matt. 16:17)
      2. A well of filling — "she filled the bottle"
      3. A well of sharing — "and gave unto the lad"

III. A WELL OF RESTORATION (Gen. 29:1, 2)
   A place of refreshment
      1. It was in the field
      2. Three flocks of sheep were by it
      3. The sheep were watered from it

IV. A WELL OF ADORATION (Num. 21:16, 17)
   A. The well is personified — "Sing ye unto it"
   B. It was the gathering center of Israel

V. A WELL OF PRESERVATION (II Sam. 17:17-19)
   A. They went down into the well
   B. They were completely covered — "Buried with Christ in baptism" (Ex. 33:22; Col. 3:3) — Sealed with the Holy Spirit

CONCLUSION:

A. W. P.

GLORYING IN THE CROSS
Galatians 6:14

INTRODUCTION:

I. GLORYING IN THE PERSON OF THE CROSS — CHRIST
  A. A living Christ
  B. A loving Christ
  C. A longing Christ

II. GLORYING IN THE PURPOSE OF THE CROSS — CREATION
  A. Creation of a new man
  B. Creation of a new manner
  C. Creation of a new motive

III. GLORYING IN THE POWER OF THE CROSS — CRUCIFY
  A. Crucifixion of a Saviour
  B. Crucifixion of sin
  C. Crucifixion of self

IV. GLORYING IN THE PROMISE OF THE CROSS — CROWN
  A. A crown of salvation
  B. A crown of security
  C. A crown of service

CONCLUSIONS:

PAUL'S POD OF "PEAS"
I Corinthians 16:1

INTRODUCTION:

I. PERIODIC — "Upon the *first* day of the week."

II. PERSONAL — "let every *one* of you."

III. PROVIDENT — "lay by him *in store*."

IV. PROPORTIONATE — "as God hath *prospered* him."

V. PREVENTIVE — "that there be *no gatherings* when I come."

CONCLUSION:

H. L. W.

DEEP CALLETH UNTO DEEP
Psalm 42:1-7

INTRODUCTION:
1. Key words — my soul, my God
2. Natural phenomenon

I. MAN'S SOUL IS A GREAT DEEP
   A. Great depth of *need*
      1. "My soul thirsteth"
      2. "Darkness on the face of the deep"
      3. Empty
   B. Great depth of *possibility*, Ps. 64:4
      1. Pain or pleasure
      2. Weal or woe
      3. Full capabilities
   C. Great depth of *responsibility*
      1. Immortal spirit
      2. Eternal consequences involved

II. GOD IS A GREAT DEEP
   A. His *thoughts* are deep, Ps. 92:5; Isa. 55:8, 9
   B. His *wisdom* and *knowledge* are deep, Rom. 11:33, 34
   C. His *love* is deep, Eph. 3:18, 19
   D. His *resources* are deep, Ps. 78:8-15

III. ONE DEEP CALLETH UNTO THE OTHER
   A. Man's emptiness calls for God's fullness
   B. The gulf between
   C. God's fullness calls for man's emptiness

CONCLUSION:
"Launch out into the deep"
"Dwell deep"

H. O. P.

PRIVILEGES AND POWER OF SERVICE
Isaiah 49:1-3

INTRODUCTION:

I. THE PRIVILEGE
   A. Called — "The Lord hath called me"
   B. Named — "He hath mentioned my name"
   C. Claimed — "Thou art *My* servant"
   D. Sheltered — "In the shadow of His hand hath He hid me"
   E. Honored — "In *whom* I will be glorified"

II. THE PREPARATION
   A. Polished — "Made me a polished shaft"
   B. Sharpened — "Made my mouth like a sharp sword"
   C. Readied — "In His quiver hath He hid me"

III. THE PURPOSE
   A. To serve Him — "My *servant*"
   B. To glorify Him — "I will be glorified"

CONCLUSION: H. O. P.

CHRIST IN THE MIDST OF THE CHURCHES
Revelation 1:12-20

INTRODUCTION:

I. THE VISION — "Candlesticks"
   A. Bearers of knowledge
   B. Bearers of holiness
   C. Bearers of benevolences

II. THE VESSELS — "Golden"
   A. Precious
   B. Purity
   C. Perpetuity

III. THE VITALITY — "Son of man"
   A. Antiquity — "white head"
   B. Garment — "priestly and judicial"
   C. Eyes — purity of fire
   D. Feet — Brass — foundation
   E. Voice — (thunder) — majesty

CONCLUSION: D. N. J.

61

AN INTRODUCTION TO THE REVELATION
Revelation 1:1-8

INTRODUCTION:

I. THE GREAT SUBJECT — "Revelation of Jesus Christ"
  A. His person
  B. His power
  C. His promise

II. THE GREAT OBJECT — "To show unto his servants"
  A. To show their faith
  B. To show their fruit
  C. To show their future

III. THE GRACIOUS BENEDICTION — "Blessed is he that readeth"
  A. Because of the tidings
  B. Because of the testimony
  C. Because of the time

IV. A CHEERY SALUTATION — "Grace and peace unto you"
  A. Salvation — Grace
  B. Justification — Peace
  C. Sanctification — Spirit

V. AN OUTBURST OF ADORATION — "Unto him that loved us"
  A. For His affection — "loved"
  B. For His purification — "washed"
  C. For His transformation — "made"

VI. A SAD LAMENTATION — "All shall wail"
  A. Determination — "all shall"
  B. Condemnation — "wail"
  C. Damnation — "forever"

VII. A SOLEMN DECLARATION — "I am Alpha and Omega"
  A. Origination
  B. Continuation
  C. Consummation

CONCLUSION:

G. H.

TENTS PITCHED TOWARD SODOM
Genesis 13:5-13

INTRODUCTION — History of a backslider:
  A. One turned from faith
  B. One seeking self glory

I. LACK OF DELIBERATION — "pitched tent toward Sodom"
  A. Started with covetousness
  B. Walked by sight
  C. Influenced by appearances

II. EVIDENCE OF EVIL PARTICIPATION — "sat in the gate of Sodom" Gen. 19:1
  A. Became a companion of the Sodomites
  B. Became a partner with the Sodomites
  C. Shown by the vanity of his testimony, "he seemed as one that mocked," Gen. 19:14
  D. Showed reluctance to leave the Sodomites, "he lingered," Gen. 19:16

III. ENUNCIATION OF DESTRUCTION RECEIVED, "For we will destroy this place," Gen. 19:13
  A. Destruction of plans
  B. Destruction of purposes
  C. Destruction of possessions
  D. Destruction of potentialities

IV. REQUISITION OF SUBSTITUTION, Gen. 19:19 (The mount of refuge too far away)
  A. Wished to be saved near Sodom
  B. Satisfaction substituted for separation

CONCLUSION:
  1. Lot enjoyed divine favor.
  2. Lot hindered God's purpose.

THE CHRISTIAN WALK

INTRODUCTION:

I. WALK BEFORE ME (Gen. 17:1)
(As children — Eph. 5:8)
   A. There is security —
      The Father is just behind (Matt. 28:20)
   B. There is assurance
   C. In full view of Him —
      Indicative of boldness

II. WALK AFTER THE LORD (Deut. 13:4)
(As a servant follows His Master)
   A. Follow wherever He leads
   B. To conform to His pattern of life (Rom. 12:2)
   C. To be present for His command

III. WALK WITH GOD (Gen. 5:24; 2:9)
(Indicates fellowship and friendship)
   A. Experiences in Eden
   B. He called us friends (John 15:13-15)
      1. Manifests love
      2. Demands service
      3. Brings revelation

IV. WALK YE IN HIM (Col. 2:6)
(Denotes union — "as members of His body")
   A. Denotes our relationship —
      1. To the world (Gal. 6:14; 2:20; Col. 3:3)
      2. To each other (Rom. 12:4, 5)
      3. To Christ (I Cor. 6:15)

CONCLUSION:

A. W. P.

GOD'S SEARCH FOR A MAN
Ezekiel 22:23-31

INTRODUCTION:

"For what kind of man does God search?"

I. GOD SEARCHES FOR MEN WHO POSSESS DEFINITE CONVICTIONS
(It makes a difference what men believe!)
   A. Men who stand for something
   B. Men who stand against something
      1. Convictions should be based upon the Word of God
      2. Convictions should be uncompromising
         a. Doctrinal
         b. Moral
      3. Convictions should be bold (Acts 4:13)
      4. Convictions should be clothed in love

II. GOD SEARCHES FOR MEN WHO EXHIBIT EXEMPLARY LIVES
(I Tim. 4:12).
   A. Word, charity, faith, spirit (humility)
   B. Unpretentious characters
   C. Purity

III. GOD SEARCHES FOR MEN TO WHOM HE MIGHT ASSIGN A
SOLEMN TASK
   A. Proclaim a dynamic personality — Christ
   B. Interpret a colossal problem — Sin
   C. Offer an adequate sin remedy — Blood

CONCLUSION:

G. D. K.

THE BLESSINGS OF PATIENT PRAYER
Psalm 40:1-10

INTRODUCTION:

I. HE LIFTED ME UP
   A. Out of a pit
      1. In which there was darkness
         a. Ignorance
         b. Superstition
      2. In which there was danger
      3. In which there was degradation
         a. Which caused condemnation
         b. Which caused separation
         c. Which caused death
      4. In which there was despair
         a. Horrors of fear
         b. Horrors of indecisions
         c. Horrors of helplessness
   B. Out of the miry clay
      1. Out of abasement
      2. Out of a sinking position
      3. Out of a trodden-down condition

II. HE SET ME UP
   A. On a sure foundation — Rock of Ages
   B. In a new life (a new man) — Creation
   C. In a new state — Justification
      1. A supernatural state
      2. A mysterious state (John 3:7)
      3. A mutual state (Gal. 2:20)
   D. In a new business

III. HE STARTED ME UP
   A. A present establishment
   B. An indicated destiny
   C. A purposeful going

IV. HE TUNED ME UP
   A. I sing a new song
   B. I sing a joyful song
   C. I sing a song of victory
      1. Victory over Satan and sin
      2. Victory over the world
      3. Victory over self

CONCLUSIONS:

66

THE TESTS OF THE TIMES
Matthew 4:1-11

INTRODUCTION:

I. THE TEST OF INSINUATION,
"If thou be the Son of God," v. 3
Doubt:
A. Salvation
B. Security
C. Service

II. THE TEST OF STARVATION,
"Command that these stones be made bread," v. 3
A. Good for food, Gen. 3:6a
B. Goal of growth
C. Game of gods

III. THE TEST OF EXALTATION,
"The devil taketh him up into the holy city and setteth him on a pinnacle of the temple."
A. A pinnacle of position
B. A pinnacle of power
C. A pinnacle of promise

IV. THE TEST OF EVALUATION,
"All these things will I give thee, if thou wilt fall down and worship me."
A. A kingdom of worldliness *vs.* a kingdom of worthiness
B. A kingdom of worldly glory *vs.* a kingdom of heavenly honor
C. A kingdom of meaningless work *vs.* a kingdom of meaningful worship

CONCLUSION: verse 11, "Then the devil leaveth him, and *behold,* angels came and ministered unto him."

R. W. S.

A GOOD MIXER
Hosea 7:1-16

INTRODUCTION:

I. THE CONDUCT OF THE MIXER — "He hath mixed himself among the people"
   A. His association
   B. His evaluation
   C. His participation

II. THE CHARACTER OF THE MIXER — "A cake not turned"
   A. Profession without possession
   B. Position without power
   C. Person without promise

III. THE CONSEQUENCES OF THE MIXER — "Strangers devour his strength"
   A. Deception
   B. Degradation
   C. Destruction

IV. THE CURE FOR THE MIXER
   A. Recognition
   B. Separation
   C. Dedication and Consecration

CONCLUSION:

VISIONS OF CHRISTIAN VITALITY
Ezekiel 47:1-12

INTRODUCTION:

I. THE RIVER OF LIFE
   A. Its source, v. 1 — "Out of the holy place"
      1. An exalted source
      2. An emptying source
      3. An everlasting source
   B. Its course, v. 1 — "by the altar"
      1. One of death
      2. One of direction (right and south)
      3. One of decision
   C. Its force
      1. To relieve, v. 8
      2. To revive, v. 9
      3. To replenish, v. 12
      4. To refresh, v. 12
      5. To repulse, v. 11

II. THE RIVER OF THE LIVING (Progressive Leadership)
   A. The Spirit of faith — "ankle deep"
   B. The Spirit of prayer — "knee deep"
   C. The Spirit of power — "loin deep"
   D. The Fullness of the Spirit —"waters to swim in"
      1. Resting upon the waters
      2. Borne up by the waters
      3. Hid by the waters
      4. Waters not to be passed over

CONCLUSION:

H. O. P.

DANIEL: GOD'S MAN IN A WICKED ENVIRONMENT
Daniel 1:1-21

INTRODUCTION:
- I. DANIEL'S PRINCIPLES
  - A. Instilled by parents
  - B. Reflected in personality
  - C. Blessed by power
- II. DANIEL'S PROVING, v. 5, 6
  - A. Instigated by a royal person
  - B. Demonstrated ample provision
  - C. Promised prestige
- III. DANIEL'S PURPOSE, v. 8
  - A. Made in the right place — heart
  - B. Respected the right person — himself
  - C. Defied the wrong portion, v. 15
- IV. DANIEL'S PROMOTION, v. 9, 20, 21
  - A. Prompted by perseverance
  - B. Profitable to all the people
  - C. Permanent position

CONCLUSION:

CONSIDER YOUR WAYS
Haggai 1:3-10

INTRODUCTION:
- I. CONSIDER YOUR WAYS IN RELATION TO GOD'S CAUSE:
  - A. A people called to worship
  - B. A place consecrated to worship
  - C. A people content to wish, v. 4
- II. CONSIDER YOUR WAYS IN VIEW OF THE RESULTS OF YOUR LABORS:
  - A. Much sowing and little reaping, v. 6
  - B. Much eating and little satisfying, v. 6
  - C. Much clothing and little warming, v. 6
  - D. Much hoarding and little saving, v. 6
- III. CONSIDER YOUR WAYS IN VIEW OF THE WORK TO BE DONE:
  - A. The Lord's pleasure
  - B. The Lord's plan
  - C. The Lord's place
  - D. The Lord's power

CONCLUSION: H. O. P.

THE BLESSINGS OF THE LORD
Zephaniah 3:8-20

INTRODUCTION:

I. WHAT THE LORD HATH DONE — In the light of our own experience as Christians
   A. He hath taken away thy judgments, v. 15
   B. He hath cast out thine enemy, v. 15
   C. He is in the midst of thee, v. 15

II. WHAT THE LORD WILL DO — God is in the midst of thee.
   A. He will save, v. 17
   B. He will rejoice over thee with joy, v. 17
   C. He will rest in His love, v. 17

III. WHAT WE SHOULD DO
   A. Praise His blessed name, v. 14
   B. Fear not, v. 16
   C. Be diligent in service, v. 16

CONCLUSION:

AARON'S ROD

INTRODUCTION:

1. Its former use
2. It was formerly dead

I. IT BROUGHT FORTH BUDS (It was made alive)
   A. According to God's purpose
   B. According to God's plan
   C. According to God's power

II. IT BLOOMED BLOSSOMS (It became a thing of beauty)
   A. Beauty of spirit
   B. Beauty of life
   C. Beauty of character

III. IT BORE ALMONDS (It became a productive thing)
   A. Fruit, John 15:1-5
   B. More fruit
   C. Much fruit

CONCLUSION:

1. Placed in the altar
2. Placed in the Holy of Holies

71

PREPARING FOR SERVICE
I Peter 1:13-16

INTRODUCTION:

I. BRACING UP — "Girding the loins of your mind"
   A. Forbids wandering
   B. Fosters work
   C. Forwards worth

II. SELF-RESTRAINT — "Be sober"
   A. Subject the flesh
   B. Activate the faith
   C. Direct the force

III. TRUST IN PROVISION AND PROMISE — "Set your hope perfectly on the grace that is to be (being) brought unto you"
   A. Grace to save
   B. Grace to secure
   C. Grace to serve

IV. DISTINCT AIM AT HOLINESS — "Be ye yourselves also holy in all manner of living (in all manner of conversation)"
   A. Look at the person
   B. Recognize the purpose
   C. Conform to the pattern
   D. Begin the practice

CONCLUSION:

OUR SHEPHERD
John 10:1-18

INTRODUCTION:

I. OUR SHEPHERD RECEIVES:
   A. Those who repent
   B. Those who call
   C. Those who come
   D. Those who believe

II. OUR SHEPHERD FEEDS:
   A. The milk of the Word
   B. The meat of the Word
   C. The Bread of Life
   D. The Water of Life

III. OUR SHEPHERD LEADS: John 10:4; Ps. 23:26
   A. In a sacred path
   B. Into a path of service
   C. Into a path of sacrifice
   D. Into a path of safety

IV. OUR SHEPHERD RELIEVES:
   A. The burden of sin
   B. The yoke of servitude
   C. The broken spirit

CONCLUSION:

A MAN SENT FROM GOD
John 1:6-8

INTRODUCTION:

I. GOD SENDS A FORERUNNER
   A. The greatness of his personality —
      "Among those born of woman"
   B. The excellency of his preaching —
      "A burning and a shining light"
   C. The supremacy of his prophecy —
      "What went ye out to see?"

II. GOD SENDS A FAITHFUL WITNESS
   A. He bore witness of Christ
   B. His witness was consistent
   C. His witness was constant

III. GOD SENDS A FULLY INSTRUCTED WITNESS
   A. Instructed about the person of Christ
   B. Instructed about the power of Christ
   C. Instructed about the pre-eminence of Christ

IV. GOD SENDS A FORCEFUL WITNESS
   A. Because of the holiness of his life
   B. Because of the wholesomeness of his light
   C. Because of the honor of his leadership

CONCLUSION:

THE EXALTATION OF ESTHER
Esther 2:1-20

INTRODUCTION:

I. HER CONDITION, v. 7
   A. Orphaned by parents
   B. Obscured by poverty
   C. Offered prospect

II. HER CALL, v. 8
   A. By providence
   B. To provision
   C. For a purpose

III. HER CHARACTER, v. 9
   A. A pleasing personality
   B. A perfect preparation
   C. A passive part

IV. HER CROWN, v. 15-17
   A. The choice of the person
   B. The crown of privilege
   C. The choice made public, v. 18

V. HER CONQUEST, 5:1-3
   A. Consecrated to the problem
   B. Courage for the place, 4:16
   C. Cast with the people
   D. Challenged by the prospect, I Peter 1:9

CONCLUSION:

O, YE OF LITTLE FAITH
Matthew 6:30; 8:26; 14:31; 16:7, 8

INTRODUCTION:

I. A REBUKE OF CARE — Matt. 6:30
   - A. Improper evaluation
   - B. Misdirected consideration
   - C. Natural limitation
   - D. Unused appropriation

II. A REBUKE OF FEAR — Matt. 8:26
   - A. Unconscious of the divine presence
   - B. Unaware of the divine purpose
   - C. Unreliant upon the divine power

III. A REBUKE OF DOUBT — Matt. 14:31
   - A. Doubting the word of Christ, 14:27
   - B. Doubting the will of Christ, 14:29
   - C. Doubting the walk of Christ, 14:30

IV. THE REBUKE OF REASONING — Matt. 16:7, 8
   - A. The place of the reasoning — "among yourselves"
   - B. The people of the reasoning — "Do ye not understand"
   - C. The production of the reasoning — "Not understand"

CONCLUSION:

SLEEPERS
Jonah 1:1-6

INTRODUCTION: Physical drowsiness deters progress. Spiritual drowsiness is set out clearly in the book of Jonah. It is the story of:

I. A DOOMED MULTITUDE
   A. A disturbing proclamation — "their wickedness is come up before me"
   B. Destructive information — The Lord told Jonah to inform Nineveh of her destruction
   C. Decisive doom — Six hundred thousand were doomed in Nineveh. Doom hangs over the world today. Atomic warfare. A billion people have never heard of Jesus. "Is it nothing to you, all ye that pass by?"

II. A DREAMING MESSENGER
   A. Jonah — unaware of the *danger* to the ship, travelers, and himself. Took a heathen shipmaster to point out the peril.
   B. A *dulled* conscience to human need. The sleeping "Christian" is in as much *danger* as the *doomed* sinner.
   C. It is a fearful thing to flee from God in *disobedience*.

III. A DECISIVE MINORITY
   A. *Surrender* of the man — God is not dependent upon vast numbers to start a revival. One alert saint can turn the tide and save a multitude.
   B. *Service* of the messenger — Keep alert by active obedience.
   C. *Sent* a *second* time to proclaim.

CONCLUSION:

CHRIST: OUR BEST FRIEND
Proverbs 17:17; 18:24; John 15:13-15

INTRODUCTION: A friend is one who knows all about us and loves us *in spite* of it. Christ shows His friendship for us by the fact that:

I. HE REASONS WITH US:
   A. About our sins, Isa. 1:18
   B. About our salvation, Matt. 11:28
   C. About our security, John 10:27, 28
   D. About our sanctification, Matt. 5:20
   E. About our service, Matt. 4:19

II. HE RESIDES IN US, I Cor. 6:19, 20
   A. To protect us, I John 4:4
   B. To be our Partner in life
   C. To empower us, I John 2:20
   D. To encourage us, Phil. 4:13

III. HE REVEALS TO US
   A. The plan of salvation
   B. The path of righteousness
   C. The place of service
   D. The prospect before us, I Cor. 2:9, 10

IV. HE REACHES THROUGH US
   A. To save men, I Cor. 1:21
   B. To share His joy of accomplishment
   C. To show our partnership with Him, I Cor. 3:9

V. HE RESERVES FOR US
   A. A sure inheritance, I Peter 1:4
   B. A satisfying portion, Ps. 17:15
   C. A standing as Princes of God, Rev. 22:5

CONCLUSION:

H. C.

78

I AM NOT ASHAMED
Romans 1:16

INTRODUCTION:
- A. To believe it
- B. To live it
- C. To practice it

I. OF THE PERSON OF THE GOSPEL
- A. His character
- B. His compassion
- C. His commands

II. OF THE POWER OF THE GOSPEL
- A. Creating power
- B. Sustaining power
- C. Translating power

III. OF THE PEOPLE OF THE GOSPEL
- A. He loves all, John 3:16
- B. He died for all, Heb. 2:9
- C. He will save all, II Peter 3:9

IV. OF THE POSSIBILITIES OF THE GOSPEL
- A. Salvation from something
- B. Salvation with something
- C. Salvation to something
- D. Salvation for something

V. OF THE PLAN OF THE GOSPEL
- A. Not all could understand
- B. Not all could work
- C. Not all could buy
- D. *All could believe*

CONCLUSION:

H. C.

79

HOW TO PRAY
Luke 11:1-4

INTRODUCTION:

    I. PRAY AS SONS — "Our Father" — RELATIONSHIP

    II. PRAY AS SAINTS — "Hallowed be thy name" — WORSHIP

    III. PRAY AS SUBJECTS — "Thy kingdom come" — KINGSHIP

    IV. PRAY AS SERVANTS — "Thy will be done" — WORKMANSHIP

    V. PRAY AS SEEKERS (BEGGARS) — "Give us day by day" — HEIRSHIP

    VI. PRAY AS SINNERS — "Forgive us our sins" — FELLOWSHIP

    VII. PRAY AS STRENGTHLESS ONES — "Lead us not into temptation" — FOLLOWSHIP — Discipleship

CONCLUSION:

J. A. F.

THE CHRISTIAN RACE
I Corinthians 9:24

INTRODUCTION:

    I. THE RACE, v. 24 — The Christ life
- A. Qualification — faith
- B. Progression — "I press," Phil. 3:13, 14
- C. Continuation — "Toward the mark"

    II. THE RUNNERS, v. 26 — The Contestants
- A. Concentration — "One thing I do"
- B. Consecration — "Lay aside every weight and sin"
- C. Dedication — "the high calling of God"

    III. THE RULES, v. 25, 27
- A. Subjection — v. 27; II Tim. 2:5
- B. Retrospection — "forgetting"
- C. Prospection — "reaching forth"

    IV. THE REWARDS, v. 25b
- A. Reception — "receiveth the prize"
- B. Coronation — "an incorruptible crown" I Peter 5:4; II Tim. 4:7, 8
- C. Jubilation — "a cloud of witnesses" — Heb. 12:1

CONCLUSION:

THE CHRISTIAN'S WALK
Colossians 1:9-12

INTRODUCTION:

I. THE MANNER OF THE WALK
   A. According to God's will, v. 9
   B. According to God's wisdom, v. 9
   C. Worthy of the Lord, v. 10

II. THE MOTIVE OF THE WALK
   A. To please God, v. 10
   B. To produce fruit, v. 10
   C. To increase in knowledge, v. 10

III. THE MEANS OF THE WALK
   A. A proper beginning — faith, v. 4
   B. A powerful energy — prayer, v. 9
   C. A plentiful source — knowledge, v. 9
   D. A personal guide — Spirit, v. 4

IV. THE MEASURE OF THE WALK
   A. Spiritual strengthening, v. 11
   B. Growth in Christian graces, vv. 11, 12
      1. Patience
      2. Long-suffering
      3. Joy
      4. Thanksgiving
   C. Made meet to be partakers of an inheritance

CONCLUSION:

TIME TO MOVE
Deuteronomy 2:1-7

INTRODUCTION:

I. THE CHECK — "Ye have compassed this mountain long enough"
   A. The satisfaction — "compassed"
   B. The duration — "long"
   C. The limitation — "enough"

II. THE COMMAND — "Turn you northward"
   A. Diversion — "Turn"
   B. Direction — "Northward"
   C. Expectation — "Land of Promise"

III. THE CAUTION — "Ye are to pass through the coast of your brethren, the children of Esau; meddle not with them."
   A. A possessed land
   B. A providing people
   C. A patient God

IV. THE COMPASSION —
   A. His favor — "The Lord thy God hath blessed thee in all the works of thy hand."
   B. His wisdom — "He knoweth thy walking through this great wilderness"
   C. His presence — "The Lord thy God hath been with thee"
   D. His provision — "Thou hast lacked nothing."

CONCLUSION:

THE RELEASE OF THE JEWS
Ezra 1:1-11

INTRODUCTION:

I. THE SUBJECTS
   A. Captives of a foreign power
   B. Controlled by a faithless person
   C. Committed to a futile purpose

II. THE AGENTS
   A. Called of God, Isa. 44:24; 45:6
   B. Conquered the oppressors
   C. Completed the operation

III. THE EXTENT
   A. Release offered to all
   B. Release accepted only by some
      1. Many did not feel any privation or degradation in their exile and subjection
      2. Many had attachments and interests in Babylon

IV. THE OBJECT — "Go up to build the house of the Lord."
   A. Universal realization of the presence of God
   B. Universal presentation of the worship of God
   C. Universal acceptance of the power of God

CONCLUSION:

THREE HOSANNAS
Matthew 21:1-16

INTRODUCTION:

  I. HOSANNA TO A FAITHFUL PROPHET
    A. His word fulfilled, vv. 2, 6, 7
    B. His work finished, vv. 4, 5
    C. His worth foretold, vv. 10, 11

  II. HOSANNA TO A HUMBLE KING
    A. His meekness indicated, v. 5
    B. His majesty vindicated, v. 12
    C. His mystery revealed, v. 16

  III. HOSANNA TO A ZEALOUS PRIEST
    A. The work established, vv. 12, 13
    B. The written word preached, vv. 13, 16
    C. The woe of his enemies pronounced, vv. 15, 16

CONCLUSION:

ISAIAH'S VIEWS
Isaiah 6:1-12

INTRODUCTION:

  I. THE VIEW FROM ABOVE — Conception of God, vv. 1-3
    A. Comfort of God's supremacy
    B. Confidence in God's exaltation
    C. Counsel of God's holiness
    D. Completeness of God's glory

  II. THE VIEW FROM WITHIN — Conviction of self, vv. 4-7
    A. Conviction of sin, v. 5
    B. Confession of sin, v. 5
    C. Cleansing from sin, vv. 6, 7

  III. THE VIEW FROM WITHOUT — Call of the world, vv. 8-12
    A. Call to service, v. 8
    B. Consecration of self, v. 8
    C. Communication to the world, vv. 9, 10

CONCLUSION:

THE MARRIAGE SUPPER
Matthew 22:1-13

INTRODUCTION:

I. THE PURPOSE OF THE FATHER
   A. His intention — "a marriage for his son," v. 2
   B. His invitation — "call them that are bidden," v. 3
   C. His insistence — "again, he sent forth other servants," v. 4

II. THE PROPENSITIES OF THE CALLED
   A. They were indifferent — "made light of it," v. 5a
   B. Their involvement — "and went their own ways," v. 5b
   C. Their insolence — "slew them," v. 6

III. THE POWER OF THE FATHER
   A. His indignation — "He was wroth"
   B. His inalterable decree — "Destroy those murderers"
   C. His incisive judgment — "Burn their cities"

IV. THE PERSISTENCE OF THE FATHER, vv. 8-10

V. THE PRONOUNCEMENT OF THE FATHER, vv. 11-14
   A. The inspection — "to see the guests"
   B. The insufficiency — "having no garment"
   C. The inability — "he was speechless"
   D. The isolation — "outer darkness"

CONCLUSION:

THE PARABLE OF THE SOWERS
Matthew 13:24-30

INTRODUCTION:

I. THE PLACE OF CULTIVATION — "The field is the world," v. 38
   - A. One of great proportion
   - B. One of dense population
   - C. One of possible improvement
   - D. One of probation
   - E. One of peril

II. THE PERSONS FOR DISSEMINATION, vv. 38, 39
   - A. The Prince of Heaven
   - B. The Prince and power of the air

III. THE PLANTS' PRODUCTION, v. 26
   - A. A prevailing mixture
   - B. An ever-present problem

IV. THE SERVANTS' RECOMMENDATION, v. 28
   - A. Only the present viewed
   - B. The personal feelings
   - C. The powerful attitude

V. THE PROPRIETOR'S DECLARATION, v. 29
   - A. Problems of discrimination
   - B. Purposes of divinity
   - C. Plans of God vs. the actions of men

VI. THE PLANT-TARES' CONSUMMATION
   - A. The harvest
     1. Predicted
     2. Certain
     3. Awful
   - B. Angels will be administrators of divine judgment
   - C. Doom of the wicked will be fearful
   - D. The destination of the righteous will be glorious

CONCLUSION:

JONAH: THE PARTING PREACHER
Jonah 1:1-3

INTRODUCTION:

I. JONAH'S IDENTIFICATION
   A. Son of an obscure man — Amittai
   B. Servant and prophet of the Lord, II Kings 14:25
      1. A personal revealer — Author
      2. A powerful witness
   C. A sovereign messenger — "Dove"

II. JONAH'S OBLIGATION — "Arise, go to Nineveh, that great city, and cry against it."
   A. The procedure — "Arise — go"
   B. The problem — "that great city"
      1. The wickedness
      2. The weakness
   C. The preacher — "a pebble against the population"
   D. The preaching — "against it"

III. JONAH'S PROCRASTINATION
   A. Displeasure at the call
   B. A downward course chosen
   C. Darting in the wrong direction

CONCLUSION:

87

JONAH: THE PLAGUED PREACHER
Jonah 1:4-7

INTRODUCTION:

I. THE SLEEPING PROPHET
   A. Out of place
      1. Dreaming in the midst of danger and desperation
      2. Helpless and useless
      3. A positive hindrance to others
   B. Without prayer
   C. Out of power

II. THE AROUSING PLEA — "What meanest thou, O sleeper; arise and call upon thy God."
   A. A plea of the heathen
   B. A point of disappointment
   C. A plan of action

III. THE OVERRULING PROVIDENCE — "the lot fell on Jonah."
   A. The Finder — God
   B. The folly of fleeing
   C. The foolish found

IV. THE STIRRING, PITIFUL POSITION
   A. The pressure of the Spirit's absence
   B. A powerless preacher in the presence of the heathen
   C. A source of perplexity

CONCLUSION:

THE REBUKES OF GRACE
II Corinthians 9:1-15

INTRODUCTION:

I. GRACE REBUKES NARROW GIVING
   A. Based upon God's love, v. 7
   B. Bound by our liberality, vv. 11, 13
   C. Blessed by God's lesson, vv. 6, 10

II. GRACE REBUKES NARROW LIVING, vv. 8, 12
   A. Abundant living made possible, John 10:10; II Cor. 8:9
   B. Ample provision promised, Phil. 4:19
   C. Attainable power for the people, I John 5:4

III. GRACE REBUKES NARROW PRAYING
   A. Man sees God's willingness
   B. God sees man's want
   C. The scope is wide — "all grace"

CONCLUSION:

JONAH: A BURIED BROTHER
Jonah 1:17; 2:1-10

INTRODUCTION:

I. THE BROTHER'S SYMBOL — a sign of the sinner
   A. Deliberate disobedience, 1:3
   B. Conviction, 2:5
   C. Confession, 2:3
   D. Prayer, 2:1
   E. Deliverance, 2:10
      1. Going away from God — "He paid the fare thereof"
      2. Coming back to God — "He had a free passage"
   F. Thanksgiving, 2:9

II. THE BROTHER'S SIGN — a sign of Christ
   A. In his burial
   B. In his conscious activity in the place of death, I Peter 3:19
   C. In his resurrection

CONCLUSION:

89

JONAH: A DISCIPLE IN THE DEEP
Jonah 1:8-16

INTRODUCTION:

I. JONAH IS SEARCHED
   A. The questioning:
      1. What is thine occupation?
      2. Whence comest thou?
      3. What is thy country?
      4. Of what people art thou?
      5. *Why hast thou done this?*
   B. The answer — "I am an Hebrew and fear the Lord God of Heaven."

II. JONAH IS SURRENDERED — "Take me up and cast me forth into the sea;"
   A. He acknowledges guilt
   B. He recognizes vengeance
   C. He accepts God's way — (The sailors attempt works, v. 13; v. 5)

III. JONAH IS SACRIFICED — "then they took up Jonah and cast him into the sea, and the sea ceased from her raging."
   A. Jonah became a substitute
   B. Jonah became a sign
   C. Jonah inspired service, v. 16

CONCLUSION:

JONAH: THE PROCLAIMING PROPHET
Jonah 3:1-10

INTRODUCTION:

I. THE REPEATED CALL — "the word of the Lord came unto Jonah a second time"
   A. The goodness of God indicated
   B. The manner of God related — "The word came" — *first*
   C. The grace of God vindicated
      1. The first call — "Cry against it" — a type of the Law
      2. The second call — "The preaching that I bid thee" — a type of the dispensation of *Grace*

II. THE READY CONCURRENCE — "Jonah arose and went"
   A. An early and easy obedience
   B. An earnest obedience
   C. An earned obedience

III. A REVEALING CRY — "Yet forty days, and Nineveh shall be overthrown"
   A. A revelation of God
   B. A revelation of grace — "forty days"
   C. A revelation of judgment

IV. A RENEWED CRIER
   A. Jonah was a confirming sign, Luke 11:30
      1. They heard his message
      2. They saw his life
   B. Jonah was a subtle contradiction to the skeptic
      1. Incarnation
      2. Regeneration
      3. Inspiration

V. A CLIMACTIC RESULT — "Nineveh repented at the preaching."
   A. They repented
   B. They believed
   C. They prayed — "Cried unto the Lord"
   D. They found mercy

CONCLUSION:

JONAH: THE DISAPPOINTED DISCIPLE
Jonah 4:1-6

INTRODUCTION:

I. HIS PLAIN LACK OF PLEASURE — "It displeased Jonah exceedingly"
   A. The prospect of the downfall of the enemies of Israel
   B. The personal problems versus the purposes of God
   C. The power of the preacher to be questioned

II. HIS PATIENT PETITION — "He prayed unto the Lord"
   A. A perfection of the unholy passion
   B. A correction of the creeds
   C. A revelation of reason

III. HIS PRAYERFUL PROFESSION
   A. Personal acknowledgment, "I knew"
   B. Powerful attributes, "gracious, merciful, slow to anger, kind, ready"
   C. Promising pardon, "turn from judgment"

IV. HIS PERSONAL PREFERENCE — "take my life — it is better for me to die than to live"
   A. A manifestation of self
   B. A declaration of faith
   C. A revelation of service

V. HIS POSITION OF PROSPECT — "so Jonah went out of the city"
   A. One of distinct separation, "out of the city"
   B. One of patient provocation, "to see what God will do"

VI. HIS PROVIDED PROTECTION — "The Lord prepared a gourd, and made it come up over Jonah"
   A. Brought jubilation, "He was exceedingly glad"
   B. Brought protection
      1. A shadow over his head
      2. A deliverance from his grief (a sign of the cross)

CONCLUSION:

JONAH: THE SILENCED SERVANT
Jonah 4:7-11

INTRODUCTION:

I. A SHORT LIVED PLEASURE, v. 7
   A. A provided pleasure
   B. A tested protection
   C. A divined purpose

II. AN OVERWHELMING PROBLEM, v. 8
   A. A severe test
   B. A serving test (a reminder)
   C. A securing test (makes one grow downward)

III. A POINTED PROPOSITION, v. 9
   A. An abiding principle — sin worketh death:
      1. In the individual
      2. In the nation
   B. An unfailing promise — righteousness exalteth a nation

IV. A SILENCING PRONOUNCEMENT
   A. An argument of sovereignty
   B. An argument of sympathy
      1. 120,000 babies involved
      2. Much cattle (property) which might be turned to the Lord's use

CONCLUSION:

FOUR LITTLE THINGS
Proverbs 30:24-28

INTRODUCTION:

I. ANTS — THE WISDOM OF PREPARATION
(Examples of industry — They are wise — There is a summer to be followed by a winter of poverty)
A. Prepare *to live* (the worth of living)
B. Prepare *to learn* (learn to work)
C. Prepare *to love* (the wisdom of loving)

II. CONIES — THE NECESSITY OF PRECAUTION
A. Take precaution with *time*
B. Take precaution with *talent*
C. Take precaution with *treasure*
D. Take precaution with *temper*

III. LOCUST — THE SECRET OF POWER
(No recognized king — Unity — Cooperation)
A. Unity in the community
B. Unity in the country
C. Unity in the church

IV. SPIDER — THE FRUITS OF PERSEVERANCE
(A loathsome spider in a palace — "The spider taketh hold with her hands.")
A. Persevere in faith
B. Persevere with facts
C. Persevere in fun

CONCLUSION:

RUTH, REDEEMED AND RECEIVED
Ruth 4:1-8

INTRODUCTION:
1. Boaz's interecession for Ruth
2. The type of the law
3. Ruth — the real treasure

I. THE PERSON OF THE REDEEMER — BOAZ
   A. His position — alone
   B. His power — able
   C. His promise — always

II. THE PURCHASE OF THE REDEMPTION
   A. It was public
   B. It was plenteous — himself
   C. It was promising — "the gleaner, through grace, becomes an heir to His glory"

III. THE PURPOSE OF THE REDEMPTION, v. 10
   A. Establishes friendship
   B. Establishes fellowship
   C. Establishes followship

IV. THE PERFECTION OF THE REDEMPTION, v. 13, "the man will not be at rest until he hath finished the thing," 3:18
   A. A present redemption — "the day of the Gentiles"
   B. The position of the redeemed — "waiting, working, watching"
   C. The possession of the redeemer

CONCLUSION:

PRAYER

INTRODUCTION:

   I. THE PLACE OF PRAYER (Matt. 6:6)

  II. THE PERIOD OF PRAYER (Luke 18:1)

 III. THE PERSON OF PRAYER (Jer. 33:3)

 IV. THE PURPOSE OF PRAYER (Matt. 26:41)

  V. THE PRIVILEGE OF PRAYER (James 5:16)

 VI. THE PROMISE OF PRAYER (John 15:7)

VII. THE POWER OF PRAYER (Rom. 10:1)

A PRAYER OF JESUS
John 17:20

INTRODUCTION: A high-priestly prayer

  I. A PRAYER FOR HIS DISCIPLES
    That they might be:
    A. Sanctified (v. 16)
    B. Successful (v. 20)
    C. Successive (v. 20)

 II. A PRAYER FOR UNITY —
    Spiritual unity:
    A. Among the disciples (v. 21)
    B. With Father and Son (v. 21)
    C. Be complete (v. 23)

III. A PRAYER FOR THE WORLD —
    That they might:
    A. Know His mission (v. 23)
    B. Know the Father's love (v. 23)
    C. Believe on Christ (v. 21)

CONCLUSION:

PRIVATE PRAYER
Matthew 6:6, 7

INTRODUCTION: Jesus Christ was preeminently a Man of prayer. He teaches us by example and precept.

I. THE PEOPLE TO PRAY — "But thou"

II. THE PERIOD OF PRAYER — "When thou prayest"

III. THE PLACE OF PRAYER — "Enter into thy closet"

IV. THE PRIVACY OF PRAYER — "Shut thy door"

V. THE PRIVILEGE OF PRAYER — "Pray to thy Father"

VI. THE PROMISE OF PRAYER — "Shall reward thee openly"

VII. THE PLAN OF PRAYER — "Use not vain repetitions"

J. C. D.

DELIVERANCE FOR CAPTIVES
Luke 4:14-22

INTRODUCTION:
1. Christ preaching His Gospel to sinners
2. Christ giving life, light, and liberty

I. THE CONDITION OF MAN EXPOSED
   A. Men are captives
   B. Men are corrupt, Eph. 4:22
   C. Men are condemned, John 3:18

II. THE MEANS OF DELIVERANCE ENCLOSED
   A. His message
   B. His method, Rom. 10:14
   C. His motive, Rom. 10:13

III. THE BENEFITS DISCLOSED
   A. Life, John 8:12
   B. Light, John 10:10
   C. Liberty, John 8:36

CONCLUSION:

D. D. F.

THE PORTRAIT OF A CHURCH
Romans 1:1-7

INTRODUCTION:
1. No record of the founding of the church at Rome
2. Jews from Rome in Jerusalem on Pentecost
3. Possibility of converted Roman soldiers carrying the Gospel there

I. THEIR RESIDENCE — "In Rome"
   A. Distant — "Last outpost of the truth"
   B. Difficult — "The weak against the mighty"
   C. Dynamic — "throughout the whole world," v. 8

II. THEIR RELATIONSHIP — "Beloved of God"
   A. Their position — "accepted in the beloved," Eph. 1:6
   B. Their protection — "even where Satan's seat is," Rev. 2:13
   C. Their prospect — "a part of the bride of Christ"

III. THEIR RESPONSIBILITY — "Called to be saints"
   A. Their motto — Rom. 12:2
   B. Their motive — "called of Jesus Christ," v. 6
   C. Their ministration — "whole world"

CONCLUSION:

I AM RESOLVED
Philippians 3:1-17

INTRODUCTION:
I. TO FORGET THE PAST
   A. Past sins
   B. Past servitudes
   C. Past services

II. TO CONCENTRATE ON THE PRESENT
   A. To live for Christ
   B. To live with Christ
   C. To live like Christ

III. TO ANTICIPATE THE FUTURE
   A. Prayerful preparedness
   B. Powerful potentialities
   C. Precious promises

CONCLUSION:

THE CHRISTIAN RACE
Hebrews 12:1, 2

INTRODUCTION:

I. THE PERSONALITIES AT THE RACE — "A cloud of witnesses"
   A. Witnesses to saving faith — Noah, Heb. 11:7
   B. Witnesses to staying faith — Abraham, Heb. 11:8-10
   C. Witnesses to serving faith — Moses, Heb. 11:24-29
   D. Witnesses to severing faith — Joshua, Heb. 11:30

II. THE PREPARATION FOR THE RACE — "Lay aside every weight"
   A. The weight of personal opportunity — selfish
   B. The weight of public opinion — Satanic
   C. The weight of potential oppression — sinful

III. THE PERSISTENCE IN THE RACE — "Run with patience"
   A. Patient continuance, Rom. 2:7
   B. Purposeful commitment
   C. Powerful concentration

IV. THE PURPOSE OF THE RACE — "Looking unto Jesus"
   A. Look for conformity
   B. Look for consecration
   C. Look for His coming

CONCLUSION:

PAUL'S PRAYER FOR THE EPHESIANS
Ephesians 3:16-19

INTRODUCTION:

I. FOR THEIR SPIRITUAL POWER, v. 16
- A. An available resource — "according to the riches of His glory"
- B. A commendable reach — "by His Spirit"
- C. An appreciable residence — "in the inner man"

II. FOR THE INDWELLING OF A PERSON, v. 17a
- A. A cleansed habitat — "in your hearts"
- B. A channel held — "by faith"
- C. A Christ to herald

III. FOR THE ESTABLISHMENT OF A PASSION, v. 17b
- A. The objects of this love
- B. The operation of this love
- C. The opportunity of this love

IV. FOR THE INCREASE OF A PRACTICAL KNOWLEDGE, vv. 18, 19a
- A. Recognition of Christ's love in its various forms and expressions
- B. Adaptations of Christ's love to our own personal conditions
- C. Application of it in all of its practical results
- D. Manifestation of it in our daily experiences

V. FOR A DIVINE PROVISION, v. 19b
- A. Beyond the asking of men
- B. Beyond the thinking of men
- C. Beyond the power of men to provide

CONCLUSION:

THE CHRISTIAN'S RACE
Hebrews 12:1, 2

INTRODUCTION:

I. THE PERSONALITIES AT THE RACE —
"a cloud of witnesses"
  A. Friendly witnesses
  B. Faithful witnesses
  C. Forceful witnesses

II. THE PREPARATION FOR THE RACE —
"lay aside every weight"
  A. Weights hinder
  B. Weights hamper (unbalance)
  C. Weights hold

III. THE PERSISTENCE IN THE RACE — "run with patience"
  A. Patient in suffering
  B. Patient in service
    1. Seeking
    2. Teaching
    3. Watching

IV. THE PURPOSE OF THE RACE — "looking unto Jesus"
  A. The beginner of our faith
  B. The keeper of our faith
  C. The finisher of our faith

CONCLUSION:

FRUIT - BEARING
John 15:1-10

INTRODUCTION:

I. CONDITIONS
   A. Cleansing (vv. 2, 3)
   B. Abiding (vv. 4-7)
   C. Loving (vv. 9, 10, 12, 17)
   D. Obeying (v. 14)

II. METHOD
   A. Praying (vv. 7, 16)
   B. Witnessing (v. 27)
   C. Suffering (v. 20)

III. RESULTS
   A. Fruit (v. 2a)
   B. More fruit (v. 2b)
   C. Much fruit (vv. 5, 8)

IV. OBJECT
   A. To glorify the Father (v. 8a)
   B. To be Christ's disciples (v. 8b)
   C. To wear a crown (II Tim. 4:8)

CONCLUSION:

D. L. F.

Occasional

BEHOLD THY MOTHER
John 19:27

INTRODUCTION:

I. BEHOLD THY MOTHER'S LEARNING, II Tim. 1:15

II. BEHOLD THY MOTHER'S LIBERALITY, II Kings 4:8-10

III. BEHOLD THY MOTHER'S LABORS, I Sam. 2:19

IV. BEHOLD THY MOTHER'S LOVE, Exod. 2:1-8

V. BEHOLD THY MOTHER'S LONGING, Prov. 23:22-25

CONCLUSION:

W. D. T.

A MOTHER IN ISRAEL
II Kings 4:8-36

INTRODUCTION:

I. HER HOSPITALITY, v. 8

II. HER PITY, v. 9

III. HER CONTENTMENT AND PEACEFUL LIFE, v. 13

IV. HER MOTHERLY LOVE, vv. 14-17

V. HER CONFIDENCE IN DAYS OF TRIAL AND SORROW, vv. 21-24

VI. HER GREAT FAITH, v. 26

VII. HER BOUNTIFUL REWARD, v. 36

CONCLUSION:

S. C. T. R.

THE MESSAGE OF THE RESURRECTION
Matthew 28:1-15

INTRODUCTION:
1. The season of the year
2. The sad outlook

I. IT IS A MESSAGE OF POWER
   A. Power to open the grave
   B. Power to give life to Christ
   C. Power to give life eternal to believers, Rom. 3:25

II. IT IS A MESSAGE OF PROOF
   A. The sad and scattered saints needed proof that all was not lost
   B. The view of the open grave is proof of the divine nature of His resurrection
   C. The Galilean meeting gave proof to the Great Commission

III. IT IS A MESSAGE OF PRAISE, vv. 8, 9
   A. Praise because of personal assurance in the vacant tomb and angelic message
   B. Praise because of personal fellowship with Him
   C. Praise because of the Hope of their own resurrection

CONCLUSION:

A. R. R.

RESURRECTION REVELATIONS
Mark 16:1-14

INTRODUCTION:

I. THE REVELATION OF HIS PERSON
   A. A living Person
   B. A loving Person
   C. A longing Person

II. THE REVELATION OF HIS POWER
   A. Liberating power
      1. From sin
      2. From self
      3. From Satan
   B. Learning power
      1. To sacrifice
      2. To serve
   C. Locating power

III. THE REVELATION OF HIS PASSION
   A. For a lost world
   B. For a learning church
   C. For a lingering creation

IV. THE REVELATION OF HIS PROMISE
   A. The proof of His resurrection
   B. The plan of His salvation
   C. The purpose of heaven

CONCLUSION:

THE POWER OF THE RESURRECTION
Philippians 3:7-11

Introduction:

I. To Know the Person of Christ,
"That I may know him," Phil. 3:10
  A. Learning Christ, "I count all things but loss for the excellency of the knowledge of Christ Jesus my Lord," Phil. 3:8
  B. Loving Christ, "That I may win Christ," Phil. 3:8
  C. Living Christ, "And be found in him," Phil. 3:9

II. To Know the Power of Christ, Phil. 3:10; Eph. 1:18-22
  A. Liberating power, Eph. 1:19, 20
  B. Elevating power, Eph. 1:19, 20
    1. Above all distinctions of power, Eph. 1:21
    2. Above all descriptions of power, Eph. 1:21
    3. Above all dispensations of power, Eph. 1:21
  C. Subjugating power, Eph. 1:22; Rom. 5:17; I Cor. 6:3; II Tim. 2:12

III. To Know the Passion of Christ, "The fellowship of his suffering," Phil. 3:10
  A. For the groping world, Rom. 9:1-3
  B. For the growing church, Gal. 4:19; Col. 1:24
  C. For the groaning creation, Rom. 8:22, 23; Phil. 3:10; John 12:24

Conclusion:

A DISTINGUISHED LINEAGE
Matthew 1:17

INTRODUCTION:

I. THE SOLEMN PROCLAMATION OF THE GENEALOGY
   A. The death of men
   B. The demands of men
   C. The duty of men

II. THE PHYSICAL CONNECTION SHOWN BY THE GENEALOGY
   A. The spirit of the relation
   B. The service of the relation
   C. The succession of the relation

III. THE PURPOSEFUL DIFFERENCES INDICATED BY THE GENEALOGY
   A. The inclusiveness of its nature
   B. The exclusiveness of its nature
   C. The preclusiveness of its nature

IV. THE PARTIAL HISTORY REVEALED BY THE GENEALOGY
   A. The potential of a man
   B. The puniness of a man
   C. The promise of a man

V. THE PROMISED REDEEMER MANIFESTED BY THE GENEALOGY
   A. His name — Son of God — Christ
   B. His claim — Son of David — King
   C. His fame — Son of Man — Jesus

CONCLUSION:

MOTHERLY CHARACTERISTICS
Matthew 15:21-29

INTRODUCTION:

I. DISCERNING: Recognized Jesus' power, v. 22

II. PRAYING: Cried unto Him, v. 22

III. WORSHIPING: Called Him "Lord," v. 25

IV. PERSEVERING: Continued to ask, v. 25

V. HUMBLE: Willingly took lowest place, v. 27

VI. BELIEVING: Had "great faith," v. 28

VII. SUCCESSFUL: Her daughter was made whole, v. 28

CONCLUSION:

W. R.

THE ANNUNCIATION OF JESUS
Luke 1:26-38

INTRODUCTION:

I. THE PERSON OF DIVINE PURPOSE (MARY)
   A. Her place — Nazareth, v. 26
   B. Her promise — the Scriptures
   C. Her pondering
   D. Her piety
   E. Her problem

II. THE PERSON OF DIVINE PROCLAMATION (JESUS)
   A. His humanity is proclaimed, v. 31
   B. His divinity is proclaimed, v. 35
   C. His royalty is proclaimed, v. 32

III. THE POWER OF DIVINE PURPOSE
   A. A revelation of favor, v. 30
   B. A declaration of the future, v. 33
   C. A manifestation of faith, v. 38

CONCLUSION:

12/17/78
A.M.

THE BIRTHDAY OF HOPE
Matthew 1:18-25; Luke 2:1-7

INTRODUCTION:

I. THE PERPLEXITIES OF THE CASE
   A. Joseph's personal position
   B. Mary's personal problem
   C. The public's prestige
   D. God's special promise

II. THE PROVIDENCE OF GOD
   A. As seen in the prophecies of God
   B. As seen in the purposes of men
   C. As seen in the preparation of God
   D. As seen in the privation of the parents

III. THE PLACE OF THE BIRTH
   A. One of poverty — a manger
   B. One of provision — Bethlehem (The House of Bread)
   C. One of position — City of David

IV. THE PRE-EMINENCE OF THE BIRTH — among the "whole world"
   A. The power of the birth
   B. The promise of the birth
   C. The presence of the Child — Emmanuel (God with us)

CONCLUSION:

NO ROOM IN THE INN
Luke 2:1-7

INTRODUCTION:

I. THERE WAS NO ROOM IN THE INN BECAUSE OF SELF
   A. Selfish possessions
   B. Selfish profits
   C. Selfish purposes

II. THERE WAS NO ROOM IN THE INN BECAUSE OF OTHERS
   A. The personality of others
   B. The position of others
   C. The power of others

III. THERE WAS NO ROOM IN THE INN BECAUSE OF THINGS
   A. Things of sentiment
   B. Things of situation
   C. Things of sensuality

CONCLUSION:

CHRIST: THE PRESENT THAT PLEASES GOD
Luke 2:21-39

INTRODUCTION:

I. THE PURIFICATION OF THE PARENTS
   A. Their dedication to the Lord of the Law
   B. Their consecration by the Lord of the Law
   C. The consideration of the Lord of the Law

II. THE PRESENTATION OF JESUS
   A. His identification, v. 13; Ex. 13:2, 12
   B. His sanctification — "Holy"
   C. His substitution — "Lamb of God"

III. THE ANTICIPATION OF SIMEON
   A. His realization and consolation
   B. His salvation and preparation
   C. His proclamation

IV. THE REVELATION OF ANNA
   A. Her affliction and privation, v. 37
   B. Her supplications, v. 37b
   C. Her declaration, v. 38

CONCLUSION:

110

THE MASTER'S MESSAGE FOR THE MEAN
Luke 2:1-18

INTRODUCTION:

I. THE REVELATION OF THE MESSAGE, vv. 9, 10
   A. The place — in the darkness of the field
   B. The power — to destroy fear
   C. The promise — demands faith

II. THE ACCEPTATION OF THE MESSAGE, v. 15
   A. Meditation — "it came to pass"
   B. Conversation — "shepherds said"
   C. Association — "let us"

III. THE VERIFICATION OF THE MESSAGE, v. 16
   A. The transition — "angels were gone"
   B. Without hesitation — "made haste"
   C. Visitation and expectation — "they came . . . and found"

IV. THE PROCLAMATION OF THE MESSAGE, v. 17
   A. The confirmation — "they had seen"
   B. The new dispensation — "made known abroad"
   C. The specification — "this child"

V. THE APPROPRIATION OF THE MESSAGE, v. 20
   A. The exemplification — "they returned"
   B. The adoration — "glorifying and praising God"
   C. The ratification — "as it was told unto them"

CONCLUSION:

THE WISE MEN AND CHRIST
Matthew 2:1-12

INTRODUCTION: All men worship; wise men worship Christ.
- I. THEIR SIGNIFICANT DIRECTION, vv. 9, 10
  - A. A resolution of faith
  - B. A disposition of presence
  - C. A provision of guidance
- II. THEIR ABUNDANT REVELATION, v. 11
  - A. The foundation of gifts
  - B. The humiliation of the giver
  - C. The transformation of the gainer
- III. THEIR SPECIFIC CONSECRATION
  - A. The subjugation
  - B. The adoration
  - C. The presentation
    - 1. Gold — kingship
    - 2. Frankincense — priesthood
    - 3. Myrrh — suffering

CONCLUSION:

GOD WITH US
Matthew 1:23

INTRODUCTION:
- I. A PRESENCE TO HUMBLE US
  - A. In His incarnation
  - B. In His habitation
  - C. In His occupation
- II. A POWER TO ENCOURAGE US
  - A. In His temptation
  - B. In His reputation
  - C. In His resurrection
- III. A PERSON TO ADMONISH US
  - A. In His instruction
  - B. In His commission
  - C. In His exemplification
- IV. A PURPOSE TO DIRECT US
  - A. In His devotion
  - B. In His preparation
  - C. In His consummation

CONCLUSION:

112

GIFTS FOR CHRIST
Matthew 2:1-15

INTRODUCTION:

I. THE GIFT OF GOLD — a signature of His kingship
   A. He was born king of Israel
   B. He becomes king in the hearts of believers
   C. He shall be king upon the earth

II. THE GIFT OF FRANKINCENSE — a signature of His priesthood
   A. He is a mediator
   B. He is an offerer of sacrifice
   C. He is a blood-bearer

III. THE GIFT OF MYRRH — a signature of His suffering
   A. Christ suffered as a man
      1. Physically
      2. Mentally
      3. Morally
   B. Christ suffered through man
      1. Because of man's ignorance of Him
      2. Because of man's misuse of Him
      3. Because of man's rejection of Him
   C. Christ suffered because of man
      1. Because of man's alienation
      2. Because of man's suffering
      3. Because of man's blindness

CONCLUSION:

113

A CHRISTLESS CROWD
Luke 2:40-52

INTRODUCTION:

I. THE CASE OF THE CARELESS, v. 43
   A. A lack of retention
   B. A fault of recognition
   C. A fearful manifestation

II. THE CURSE OF SUPPOSITION, v. 44
   A. The pressure of their company
   B. The presence of their relatives
   C. The potential of their acquaintances

III. THE CONSEQUENCE OF THE SEARCH, v. 45a
   A. They sought the right person
   B. They searched among the wrong people
   C. They searched in the wrong place

IV. THE CURE FOR THE PERPLEXITIES, v. 45b
   A. A definite return
   B. An assuring reward
   C. A proper recognition

CONCLUSION:
   1. The crowd went on without Jesus
   2. Only Joseph and Mary returned
   3. Jesus returned only with His parents
   4. Jesus was subject to His parents — not to the crowd

114

IMMANUEL
Isaiah 7:14

INTRODUCTION:

I. AN EXPLANATION OF THIS GREAT AND EXTRAORDINARY TITLE
   A. The constitution of His person — Incarnation
   B. The office of position — mediation
      1. As a distant friend with us
      2. Appearances of Christ in the Old Dispensation
   C. The provisions of His power — redemption
      1. Naturalization and Revelation
      2. Reconciliation and Justification
      3. Sanctification and Glorification

II. THE DECLARATION OF CHRIST TO GOD'S PEOPLE
   A. He fulfills a need for them
   B. He is reason for worship
   C. He predicts their future

III. CONSIDERATION OF SOME OF THE DUTIES ARISING FROM THIS WONDERFUL FACT
   A. Adore the condescension
   B. Proclaim the doctrine of the deity of Jesus
   C. Communication with Him is desirable
   D. Recognition of His presence and position

CONCLUSION:

ONE OF WONDERFUL NAME
Isaiah 9:6, 7

INTRODUCTION:

I. THE ROYALTY OF CHRIST — "Son of David" — King
  A. By birth, Luke 2:11
  B. By bond, Luke 3:23
  C. By blood, Matt. 1:1

II. THE RIGHTS OF CHRIST — "Son of God" — Saviour
  A. Creative rights, John 1:1-3
  B. Counseling rights — Evident in His message
  C. Calling rights

III. THE REJECTION OF CHRIST — "Son of Man" — John 1:11
  A. Rejection of His virgin birth, Gen. 3:15; Isa. 7:14
  B. Rejection of His victorious life
  C. Rejection of His vicarious death

IV. THE RETURN OF CHRIST — "Father of Eternity"
  A. The promise, John 14:3
  B. The prophecy, Acts 1:11
  C. The prospect, I Thess. 4:14-18

V. THE REIGN OF CHRIST — "Prince of Peace"
  A. A recognized Prince, Isa. 9:7
  B. A resourceful peace, Isa. 9:7
  C. A restricted plan, Isa. 9:7

CONCLUSION:

GOD'S GIFT TO MEN
John 1:1-14

INTRODUCTION:

I. THE INCARNATION — "made flesh"
   A. Condescension, Phil. 2:7
   B. Humiliation, Phil. 2:8
   C. Propitiation, II Cor. 5:21

II. THE HABITATION — "among us"
   A. Recognition, John 1:12
   B. Reconciliation, II Cor. 5:18, 19
   C. Regeneration, John 1:13

III. THE REVELATION — "only begotten of the father"
   A. Affection — John 3:16
   B. Salvation — John 3:16
   C. Preservation — John 3:16
   D. Condemnation — John 3:18

IV. THE DECLARATION — "full of grace and truth"
   A. Combination and completion, Ps. 85:10; John 1:17
   B. The liberation, John 1:16-18; John 8:32
   C. The transformation, II Cor. 5:17

CONCLUSION:

117

IN THE FULLNESS OF TIME
Galatians 4:1-11

INTRODUCTION:

I. THE PROPRIETY OF THE TIME — "In the fulness"
   A. Prophecies of the Old Testament centered in Christ
   B. Productions of the world order culminated in men
   C. Preparations of the times calculated the event

II. THE PURPOSE OF THE TIME — "God sent forth his Son"
   A. His pre-existence indicated
   B. His personality revealed
   C. His presupposition of the ransom proclaimed

III. THE PERSONALITY OF THE SON — "Made of a woman"
   A. Possessor of a higher nature
   B. Points to a supernatural conception
   C. Position of the woman

IV. HIS PLACE UNDER THE LAW — "Made under the Law"
   A. Personally accepted
   B. Purposely placed
   C. Potentially secured

V. THE POWER OF THE MISSION OF THE SON —
   "To redeem them that were under the curse of the law"
   A. Under the curse of Eden's law, Rom. 8:1-3
   B. Under the curse of Moses' law, Rom. 8:1-3
   C. Under the curse of Calvary's law, Rom. 8:1-3

CONCLUSION:

THE MESSIAH'S SONSHIP
Hebrews 1:1-14; Matthew 22:41-46

INTRODUCTION:

I. HE IS THE TRUE KING — "Son of David" — Matt. 1:1
   A. According to divine purpose
   B. According to divine prophecy
   C. According to divine planning

II. HE IS THE TRUE JEW — "Son of Abraham" — Matt. 1:1
   A. The seed of Abraham, Gal. 3:16
   B. The satisfaction of Jewish believers
   C. The salvation of God — "Salvation is of the Jews"

III. HE IS THE TRUE MAN — "Son of Adam" — Luke 3:38
   A. He is the Life of men, John 1:4
   B. He is the Light of men, John 1:7
   C. He is the Lifter of men, John 12:32

IV. HE IS THE TRUE GOD — "Son of God" — Mark 1:1
   A. He is the Beginner, John 1:3
   B. He is the Begettor, John 1:12
   C. He is the Beloved, Matt. 3:17; 17:5

CONCLUSION:

SCRIPTURE INDEX